RACCOONS

RACCOONS

In Folklore, History & Today's Backyards

Virginia C. Holmgren

Capra Press

SANTA BARBARA
1990

Cover design and drawing, title page drawing,
book design, typesetting and image scanning
by Frank Goad
SANTA BARBARA, CALIFORNIA

Library of Congress Cataloging-in-Publication Data

Holmgren, Virginia C.
  Raccoons in folklore, history, and today's backyards / Virginia C.
Holmgren.
    p. cm.
  Includes bibliographical references.
  Summary: Presents facts and lore about raccoons, drawn from
  Indian legends, current scientific findings, and face-to-face
  encounters.
  ISBN 0-88496-312-8 : $10.95
  1. Raccoons--Juvenile literature. [1. Raccoons.] I. Title.
QL737.C26H64   1990
599.74'443--dc20   89-48704

PUBLISHED BY
CAPRA PRESS
POST OFFICE BOX 2068
SANTA BARBARA, CALIFORNIA 93120

TABLE OF CONTENTS

ACKNOWLEDGMENTS

Sincere thanks are hereby offered the many librarians who gave generous assistance over the more than twenty years of my research for this book. Included are the libraries of the Museum of Comparative Zoology and of the Peabody Museum of Anthropology and Ethnology at Harvard University; the Library of Congress; American Museum of Natural History; Oregon Primate Research Center; Academy of American Franciscan History; Oregon University; Oregon State University; University of Portland; Smithsonian Institution (National Zoological Park, National Museum of Natural History); New York Public Library; University of Florida; also Martha P. Ott, Curator of Archaeology, Ohio Historical Society, and—as always in my research—the Multnomah County Public Library in Portland, Oregon, especially those in charge of inter-library loans and with special thanks to Betty Johnson and Barbara Kale. My thanks also to Malcolm and Louise Loring for sharing their knowledge of Columbia River petroglyphs, to Dr. Charles Dibble of the University of Utah, Dr. Charles Handley and Dr. Theodore Reed of the National Zoo; and other raccoon watchers Jean Taylor, Richard and Doris McCann and Clyde and Lou McLean, Marger Robertson, Jane Sansregret.

ONE

A PLACE TO BEGIN

THE GRIZZLE-FURRED ANIMAL *with the bushy ringed tail paused by the stream's edge, every sense alert. Pointed ears twitched to the right, the left. The head turned slowly, showing black eyes masked by a black band of fur edged in white stretching from cheek to rounded cheek. Pointed snout ended in a black blob nose, and now nose, eyes and ears all took silent survey, seeking assurance that no scent, sight or sound of danger threatened.*

Satisfied all was safe, the masked one stepped into the shallows, found firm footing near an overhanging rock where the plumpest fish often lingered—and became like a rock himself, unmoving. Sometimes this rock trick demanded almost unendurable patience. But not today. Today a good-sized fish came nosing slowly into the shallows as if asking to be caught. Instantly the agile forepaws closed in firm grip, as he flipped the fish out onto the bank and leaped to clasp it again, slam it against the rocks until it was senseless. Suddenly he rose upright, still holding the fish close, warily eyeing a clump of bushes screening a bend in the stream. His ears had given warning of an unseen something moving just beyond the greenery and now his eyes added proof. A strange creature—with others he could not yet see following behind—came around the bend walking as easily upright as he himself did on all four. Now the two-legged ones saw him and stopped mid-stride as if taken completely by surprise, staring at him as avidly as he stared back, each assessing the other. Those who followed said something to the leader, as if asking for guidance, and he held out his hand, bidding them to wait as he stepped forward and began to speak.

Photo: Sam Dabney

"We give you greeting, mask wearer," he began in a soft tone he was sure held only friendly warmth. He had never seen an animal like this before, but like other wildlings it would know that a stranger who came openly did not intend attack. Only enemies came in silence and stealth. He would use words that told of peaceful intent, since that was the only way he could be sure his voice would carry the message. His followers would understand, too. He was sure they would notice the mask now—if they hadn't at first—and realize that this might be a Spirit Being in animal disguise. Among their tribe a mask was always a sign of magic and power. Even the most ordinary man or woman—if chosen to wear a mask in sacred ritual—would be possessed completely by the spirit animal it represented. But whether this be spirit or wildling, the message that they came in friendship must be clear.

"We are wanderers," he went on in the same calm tone. "We have come from cold northern lands of ice and snow seeking a warmer land for our home. The birds told us by their autumn flight—always southward—that this is the way we should go. Tomorrow we will go on still farther south. But now may we stay and fish in your stream to quiet our hunger? May we sleep here for the night then leave as we have come—in peace?"

Slowly the speaker stepped forward, hands extended with palms up and empty, but at the first movement the mask wearer dropped the fish and headed for the nearest thicket in a rolling, flatfoot gait. If he had waited he might have read the peaceful gesture correctly, but wild wisdom had taught him that when faced with the unknown it was safest to seek refuge and make further survey only when safety was certain. At least he was sure his eyes and ears and nose would recognize these strangers again if they came his way. For now, that was enough. . .

The two-legged ones left alone on the bank looked at their leader asking for explanation. Was this creature spirit or true animal?

"I don't know," the leader admitted. "When I saw the mask—and those paws as agile as my own two hands—I thought it was a spirit. But then it ran from us in fear and so. . ."

A shrug completed his thought.

"But he gave us the fish!" one of the children protested, pointing. "An animal wouldn't do that."

The leader smiled. "A gift is a gift," he said, "intended or not. Can you catch enough more for our meal?"

Quickly the women and children separated into groups—some to fish, others to gather wood, arrange stones for a cookfire. Still smiling, the leader turned toward the thicket where he thought the mask wearer might be keeping watch.

"Our thanks, masked one," he called out. "Our thanks to you and the Great Spirit who cares for us all."

No one knows whether this was how raccoon and human first met, but it could have happened just this way. When telling the story of the raccoon, one fact must be established right at the beginning: raccoons are native only to the Americas. The first meeting with humans had to take place on New World soil.

Where in the New World would have been the likeliest meeting place? Almost all experts who have delved into ancient American Indian history as revealed by fossil bones, and artifacts and ancient campsights believe that the first human settlers came from northern Asia to Alaska by way of a now-vanished land bridge. These were the ancestors of today's Indians and in time they wandered on—some southward, some eastward—seeking more hospitable terrain. And it was not until they made their way well to the south that they could have seen their first raccoons, for the mask wearers have never lived of their own choice where icebound winters make hunting impossible.

So somewhere not far from today's U.S.-Canadian border could well have been the place. And it could also have been on a riverbank, for both human and animal wanderers used flowing water as a reliable trail and easy source of food.

Proof of where raccoons live now is well established by frequent surveys. Where they roamed in prehistoric times has been proven by numerous excavations showing the presence of raccoon bones from the Canadian border-lands southward. By fossil testimony we know ancient Indian wanderers could have seen raccoons many places—along the banks of the Columbia River in the Pacific Northwest, down the Mississippi's full length, almost anywhere in Florida, on down to Brazil, northern Argentina, west as far as the Andes foothills. Raccoons still live in almost all these areas and on the isthmus that links the two continents and on most of the offshore islands in between. But no fossil bones have been found anywhere in New World arctic or antarctic lands or anywhere in the Old World.

Raccoon bones and Indian bones have been found

together in the Pacific Northwest beside campfires whose embers faded to gray ash at least ten thousand years ago. Farther east, one cave along the banks of the Mississippi River near St. Louis yielded raccoon bones and Indian bones side by side as the animals and humans must have lived some eight thousand years ago, according to research experts at the Illinois State Museum.

When factual evidence takes the story of raccoon and human relationship back that far, it does not really matter whether older bones of the two may someday be uncovered somewhere else. It is enough for us to be sure that in some prehistoric era of America's beginnings Native American humans had a first meeting with an animal whose American heritage is even more ancient than their own.

Anthropologists can study the physical evidence around ancient campfires, but we have further proof of Indians' interactions with raccoons preserved in their native languages. From Columbus onward, European visitors to the Americas transcribed many of the Indian words they heard—especially terms describing sights the Europeans had never experienced before. Explorers, fur traders, missionaries, sight-seeing travelers and hopeful settlers often published these vocabularies and enough of them have been preserved to furnish the animal now called "raccoon" with a whole glossary of alternate names in various tribal languages and dialects. And when the literal meaning of the name—as well as the spoken syllables in phonetic echo—is translated, we have a key that works like magic to reveal the thoughts of those who chose the name in ancient times.

Many seeing a raccoon for the first time considered the mask an identifying feature to remember and so chose "mask wearer" as the name. Others thought the agile paws or ringed tail more deserving of namesake label. Still others thought of typical actions, calling it "fish-catcher," "crab-eater," "night-rover," or described it in some other way.

Every ancient name that has survived tells us something

of the raccoon story. Legends that were heard and remembered and re-told were finally written down for permanent record, too, and have become a fascinating part of raccoon lore. Even more names and legends were added by settlers who found raccoons as unexpected frontier neighbors. For that matter, even today some city-born Americans find raccoons in suburban backyards and think up a few expressive labels not usually in zoological annals.

TWO

WHAT NAME FITS A RACCOON?

IF YOU HAD NEVER SEEN A RACCOON—never even heard of it—and one suddenly appeared, what would you call it? If this first unwarned glimpse was of a furry, black-masked face peering out of your favorite cherry tree with red juice dripping from well-stained lips, chances are good you'd burst into an irate salvo of names such as "Bandit! Burglar! Thief!" followed by "Get out! Scram!"

The black mask demands labels of villainy. Even though few of us have ever been held up by scoundrels sporting such disguise, our folklore tells us who wears it. Television, movies and oldtime romantic novels have given us so many bad guys hiding behind this black band that we don't even stop to think that mask wearers in fur do not carry guns.

It was eating your cherries. That's thievery in your book, but not in the raccoon's. Animals do not understand the human claim to exclusive property rights of such natural delights as fruit on a tree or fish in a pond. By their law—nature's law—food belongs to whoever finds it first and can hold on to it. Raccoons excel at this. They also show considerable ingenuity maneuvering under and over fences and other barricades and an uncanny talent for knowing just the very moment fruit is ripe and ready for eating—a moment that usually occurs the night before the morning on which some human had planned to arrive basket in hand.

There they are, munching away, with well-stripped branches all around while you stand below and glare. Perhaps, then, you will wonder if ancient Indians also thought the raccon mask a disguise for thieves and bandits.

Preserved in museums and by tribal traditions, Indian masks seen today are usually elaborate art objects of tanned animal skin, woven fabric or wood. These were too bulky for the wandering tribes of early days to carry with them. A smear of black soot or charred wood from the evening cookfire was always handy, however, and most primitive tribes the world around discovered that a black smear across the cheeks and over the eyes could change a face so much even a friend looked unfamiliar. Limestone for whitewash was almost as easy to provide when they camped at a favorite fishing hole or hunting grounds, and a white smear seemed to work the same magic whether used alone or in addition to the black.

So for many ancient reasons, two-fingered swashes of black or white became the standard disguise when sacred rituals demanded the submersion of an individual's identity beneath that of a Spirit Being. Raccoons who wear that same disguise naturally could easily be thought to have spirit powers to match. This conclusion is not mere guess work. It is proven by the many tribal names for raccoon linked to masks and their magic power of disguise.

Tribes of Sioux heritage, for instance, gave the raccoon several names researchers accept as stemming from older, half-forgotten words meaning "one who is sacred" or "one with magic." When recorded phonetically by English-speaking historians, these usually appear as *wee-kah* or *wee-chah, wee-kah-sah* or similar-sounding syllables. The same vowels may be used with an initial "m" rather than a "w." One recorder noting the name from a tribe of Dakota Sioux gave the complete label as *wee-kah teg-alega*, meaning "sacred one with painted face"—plainly a reference to the masklike marking.

The "paint" was often recorded as two-colored, usually black and white, with the translator describing the facial patterns as pied. Sometimes there was an added word hinting at magic, too, although the mask itself was enough to suggest supernatural influence at work.

Magic was undoubtedly in the Aztecs' minds when they named the raccoons *see-oh-at-la-ma-kas-kay*. This has been translated as "she who talks with gods" and therefore was meant only for female raccoons. Another Aztec term, given only to female raccoons with kits was *ee-yah-mah-tohn* and meant "little old one who knows things." Since the mask is worn by both male and female raccoons, the facial marking was not responsible for these names. Instead, they suggest that whoever coined and used them must have been watching raccoon behavior and thereby knew that the mother tends the kits and teaches them raccoon ways. She has to "know things" or neither she nor the kits would survive. And what she knew granted her a rank that Aztecs also gave to tribal Wise Women.

In the Pacific Northwest where the Columbia River tumbles into a gorge with towering basalt cliffs on either side, an unknown Indian artist once carved the giant face of the land's guardian spirit. The face was called *tsa ga gla lal*, "she who watches." And though Yakima people living there now call it "witch

Sketch of "She Who Watches" petroglyph by author.

17

woman," or "watcher," the artist portrayed it as an animal with round face, upright ears and masklike cheek markings resembling those of a raccoon.

Anyone who knows the ways of a mother raccoon with her kits—as the ancient artist must have—soon learns that she teaches them to wait beneath the shelter of overhanging rock or surrounding greenery before venturing into an open place such as meadow or riverbank. "Wait and watch" is her lesson for survival, "wait and watch and listen and sniff" for sight or sound or scent of danger. It was a lesson that the ancient Indians themselves needed to learn, and the giant face—38 x 34 inches—would have been an ever-present reminder, as it is now for all who find it still on guard in Washington's Horsethief Lake State Park. Similar faces are carved elsewhere in the state, each one a hint that "she who watches" may well be a sister-under-the-mask to the Aztecan "she who talks with gods" and "she who knows things."

It is possible the Aztecs' special rank for females of kit-bearing years put a taboo on killing them for food or fur. Restricting hunting to male animals was customary in many primitive tribes and was mentioned among Hebrew laws in the Old Testament. And raccoons were definitely a hunted animal that might be in need of protection from time to time—especially on islands, as the first Spaniards in the Caribbean would discover very quickly.

Indian tribes valued the thick raccoon fur. Pelts, with or without the head and tail, were sewn together for warm bedding or a wraparound winter coat. The tails alone were prized as personal decoration, dangling proudly from belt or headdresss, clearly a status symbol. Sometimes the head with its mask design was also an ornament. The flesh, roasted or added to stews, was

Indian with raccoon tails: DeBry Lemoyne, 1595

counted tasty fare and the fat often was saved apart to add savor to other food and was also made into a salve valued for the comfort it gave to aching muscles, bruises, sprains. Even the bones were shaped into small tools or carved for ornaments

Raccoons were usually so plentiful—at home wherever there were woods and water—that most tribes could supply their own needs for fur and food. But in the northeast the Great Lakes came close to marking the northern limit of raccoon abundance. One tribe living on the southern shore of the southernmost of these waters made a good business of supplying furs to northern tribes. When these traders went far enough to the north, the tribes they met did not recognize the furs offered, did not even have a name for the animal in their language.

Evidently the northern tribe of Hurons were the first in the area to use their term for "big-tailed" to identify both the raccoon pelts as well as the tribes who traded the furs. Other northern tribes copied the Huron name and soon the southern traders were known almost everywhere north of the lakes as "people of the long-tailed ones." Similarly the lake marking their home boundary line was called the "lake of the long-tailed ones." French settlers and traders in the area transcribed this word phonetically as *iri* or *eri*, usually with *a-chis* added to match the Indian suffix for "of this kind." The English, however, spelled the same sounds as *ee-ree-a-gee*. Through the years the final acceptable spelling became *erie*, and today the lake, numerous towns, streets and local organizations are named Erie.

The French mistook the *iri* for the European wild cat, a wary woods animal also identified by a bushy, ringed tail. In 1612 explorer Samuel de Champlain had a map drawn complete with a sketch of a raccoon beside the lake's northern corner. This is the first time the Huron term

Detail of map, Carte Geographique, 1612.

iribachis has been found identifying both the lake and the namesake animal.

In 1690 a French geographical society published a map of North America and labeled the lake *Lac Erie ou Du Chat*, "Lake Erie Or The Cat." The southern shore was identified as the former home of the *Nation du Chat, destruites par les Iroquois*, "Nation of the Cat, destroyed by the Iroquois." Drawn on the map is a cat-faced animal, more the coloring of the beaver than a raccoon—probably the mistake of a French artist who had never seen the animal.

Detail of French map, 1690, showing *Lac Erie ou Du Chat*.

This map establishes the original meaning for Erie by those who first coined the name. Both lake and tribe are raccoon namesakes, although most local residents think Erie refers to a panther. This confusion began with early English settlers who thought the French were referring to the mountain lion, the only native long-tailed cat in the area. The English described this lion by several terms, but panther, an old Asian word, sounded fiercest. And so the misuse continues to this day.

Meanwhile, other tribes across the Americas had identified the raccoon as a relative of the dog. Down in the Bahama Islands, Taino people had one word for both dogs and raccoons, *ah-on*. They kept both as family pets and at times used both as food and were well aware that raccoons also roamed wild on many of the islands.

Tupi Indians of Brazil placed the raccoons in a group with dogs and all other animals that pounce on their prey with a crouching, all-at-once spring. Each animal in the group was called a *uara*, "leaper." You can still hear the echo of that old term in our modernized names of "cougar" and "jaguar." The basic term was modified to indicate specific "leapers." For instance, the jaguar was "leaper that kills with a single pounce." The cougar was "leaper camouflaged in the coloring of a deer." The dogs, foxes and raccoons were all categorized as *aguara*, "doglike leapers." The full term for the raccoon was *aguara-popay*, meaning "doglike leaper upon crabs and crayfish." When the Tupi talked together they sometimes omitted the full name, assuming the listener would know which leaper was in question. The Europeans were confused by so many different animals with the same name. One traveler wrote in disgust that even a kind of fish were *uaras*, not realizing that "leaping" was as reasonable a name as "flying" for a fish that takes to the air.

In the Pacific Northwest, Klamath people also thought of raccoons as doglike, but not because of their four-legged hunter's leap. For them, the raccoon was valued most of all as a friendly family pet, and so they spoke of it as a *wacgina*, "animal that can be tamed like a dog."

As Indian tribes all across the Americas came to know the raccoon better, they marveled at the remarkable, do-everything, touch-everything forepaws so similar to human hands. On the raccoon the toe in thumb position is somewhat low set, not as low as the human thumb, but low enough so that it offers at least some opposition to the other toes for an almost-human grip on whatever it wants to pick up and examine or put in its mouth for a tasty bite.

The raccoon outer toe, like a human little finger, is slightly lower than the central digits, and therefore provides additional holding power. Also raccoon paws have something human hands do not—extremely sensitive skin on the palms. The paw reaches out and with first contact it relays the message of what it has touched—familiar and good to eat, familiar and not good at all, or strange, unknown and needs further check.

Only with this last warning is there need for a raccoon to look down at what has been found. It can reach for one more grape from the vine, one more tidbit from a dog's feeding bowl and keep eyes, ears and nose trained elsewhere for hint of danger. One touch and it can drop something too difficult to eat and reach for a better tidbit. If everything within reach is too hard or dry—like stale bread crusts—raccoons use an old family trick and dunk it in the backyard birdbath or whatever water is handy. Much of a raccoon's natural food is found in or near water and dunking has been easily learned by kits ready to copy their mother. Perhaps it is even part of their inherited behavior pattern. However, individual preference is involved, too. Some raccoons dunk almost everything, hard or soft, while others dunk almost nothing.

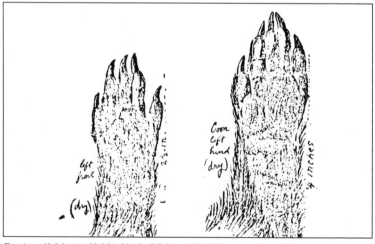

Drawings of left front and left hind feet by E.T. Seton, 1886–1909.

The toe that is almost a thumb aids the raccoons in skillful dunking. It also gives them incredible talent for opening latches, untying knots—or tying them—twisting vines into a trap or keeping firm hold on even the wiggliest worm or crayfish. Indians of long ago watched the way those agile paws solved each problem and decided these handy ones needed a name to match their talents.

The very name *raccoon* was coined for just this reason. *Ah-rah-koon-em* was the pronunciation used by Algonkin Chief Powhatan and his daughter Pocahontas. English settlers arriving in 1607 to claim Powhatan's land as their own first permanent New World colony copied it as best they could. They readily accepted the idea that an American animal unknown in the Old World should have an American name. And once they learned that the Indian word means "one who rubs, scrubs and scratches with its hands," there was no reason to change. They argued how to spell it or even how to pronounce it, but they couldn't doubt that rubbing, scrubbing, scratching—and patting, pulling thumping, twisting and turning—were part of every raccoon's routine, no matter what was picked up in those agile paws.

At least twenty or more tribal names for raccoon have much the same meaning. Each tribe had its own language, but they all observed raccoons and marveled at their manual dexterity. "They pick up things" was the translation for the name used by Cree and Chippewas. Lenape Delaware choice was "they use hands as a tool." Another Delaware tribe said "those with clever fingers." Several tribes not close enough to borrow Powhatan's name also decided to include rubbing, scrubbing or scratching when they named the raccoon. Down in Mexico the Aztecs summed up raccoon action with "they take everything in their hands." The Spanish settlers who heard it soon softened the Aztec *mapachitl* into the Spanish *mapache*. Like "raccoon" for the English-speaking, *mapache* has become the name for this American busy-fingered animal wherever Spanish is spoken.

For ancient tribal leaders, choosing animal names was a serious matter. Names with meaning, pointing out some difference in behavior, appearance or voice, would help differentiate one kind from another. Birds—often heard before they were seen—were usually given names to imitate their song or call notes. Mammals were more easily recognized by color patterns or activities. Besides name clues, memory was also aided by stories of animal ways. Sometimes these tales were serious lessons, passing along tribal wisdom. But even lessons were often lightened by a few just-for-fun incidents—especially when raccoons were involved. After all, any animal able to use its hands as a tool is bound to use them for mischief too! And Indian storytellers seldom missed a chance to give their listeners a chuckle.

Photo: Virginia C. Holmgren

THREE

WHERE THERE'S A RACCOON, THERE'S A LEGEND

STORYTELLERS IN EVERY LAND and time have always been spurred by the human need for laughter. But in primitive times, tribal storytellers realized that their people also had an ever-growing need to understand why things happen as they do in nature's world. They weren't content just to look and marvel at the changing seasons and all the many differences among plants and animals. Their survival depended on knowing the animals and predicting the seasonal changes.

"Why?" they kept asking the Wise Ones. "How did it happen?"

And because admitting ignorance is not the way Wise Ones hold onto a place of honor, they gave an answer. Sometimes they must have felt they were like weavers asked to produce cloth without yarn or pattern. But almost always their own observations and experiences had given them at least some small thread of truth and those who now read the ancient tales now learn to look for it, accept it as proof that myth and legend—for all the imaginative embroidery—were also the first attempts at scientific explanations.

Raccoons, with their masquerade faces and almost-human dexterity, were bound to stir up questions that led to answer-tales told around many an Amerind campfire. For instance, if that mask wasn't a bond with the spirits, how did raccoons come by such markings? Why were raccoons so lucky at catching fish, especially crayfish? And at finding fruit just the moment it was ripe and ready to eat? Why were they always playing tricks on other animals, getting into mischief? Which animals tried to trick raccoons?

If you'd like to hear a few answers to such questions, just imagine you're back there beside a long-ago campfire and listening. . .

How raccoons got their markings.
(A NEZ PERCE LEGEND)

Long, long ago when the world was only half begun, all furry four-legged creatures were much alike in size and shape and their earth-tone coloring. Most of them were alike in having a calm take-things-as-they-come temperament, too. But not Raccoon! And certainly not Coyote! Those two were full of mischief right from the start. Always up to tricks. Always trying to get the best of somebody with a prank or two so they could sit back and watch as matters went from bad to impossible for whoever was caught in the tangle. And of course each liked to catch the other best of all.

One night Raccoon was soft-footing it through the forest planning how he would trick Coyote if he could find him asleep. Tie his tail to a tree with a long vine, perhaps, pulling the knot so tight it would never come loose. Or plaster his eyes shut with wet clay. Plenty of the slimy stuff was always handy if Coyote was taking his usual after-supper snooze on the riverbank.

And on the riverbank sound asleep was just where Raccoon found him. Sound asleep beside the cookfire where he'd been roasting a salmon for supper. Nothing left of the fire now but black cinders. Nothing left of the salmon but bones. Seeing those bones really stirred Raccoon to action, for salmon was one of his own favorite foods.

"Hmm," he said to himself, looking around for a good sturdy length of vine. Tying knots Coyote couldn't untie was one of his best tricks. And there was just the vine he needed trailing from a big oak tree at river's edge! Quickly he started forward on tip-toe—one step, two. The next moment he was whirling through the air, for Coyote had him by the tail, the neck, the nose. What was worse, Coyote began swishing Raccoon's tail through the cinders. First in the cinders and then in the muddiest mud puddle on the riverbank. This way, that way! Back and forth until the tail was ringed round and round with bands of black and brown, black and brown—cinders and mud, cinders and mud.

"Ai! Yi!" yelped Raccoon furious with Coyote for only pretending to be asleep, and even more furious with himself for being caught by such an old trick. "Let go of me! Let go of my tail!"

"As you wish," said Coyote with pretended politeness. And he did drop the besplattered tail, reaching for a tender pointed ear with one hand, scooping up slippery white clay with the other.

Splat! Splotch! and there was one white smear above Raccoon's eyes and another on his snout just above the black blob nose.

Now Coyote changed hands, this time scooping up black cinders he swished through a mud puddle and then across Raccoon's face cheek to cheek. Splat! Splotch!

"Oh! Oh!" Coyote chortled. "Your face! Your face!"

If he hadn't been laughing so hard he would have realized that Raccoon was slipping out of his grasp, slipping clear away and inching closer and closer to the oak tree. But Coyote was all doubled over with glee, not noticing anything until Raccoon was shinnying up the tree to a high branch where Coyote couldn't possibly follow. Tree climbing was just not Coyote's trick.

"Didn't hurt me!" Raccoon boasted. "Didn't hurt me at all!" That wasn't exactly true, but he had to say it for pride's sake. Besides, he had gotten loose. In a moment he'd figure out how to get clear away.

"Ha!" Coyote snorted. "Didn't hurt you, huh? Look at your

face! I smeared clay all over it!"

Raccoon squeezed his eyes down and tried to push his cheeks up. He couldn't really see the smears but he knew Coyote wasn't lying. "Oh, clay washes off," he said trying to keep a don't-care tone in his voice.

"Not that clay!" Coyote boasted. "It's magic. And there to stay. So are those rings on your tail."

Raccoon looked back at his tail. The rings did look settled in.

"Hmm," he said, ready as usual to make the best of anything that couldn't be helped. "Rings. Rather nice rings, I think. Different."

Just then he looked down and caught a glimpse of his face reflected in the water. Different was the word, all right. No other animal in the forest had a face mask like his. He was one of a kind. Special. Special face, special tail.

And that was just the way he liked it. At least he would never give Coyote a hint he thought otherwise.

TODAY'S COMMENT

The storyteller must have wanted listeners to notice that raccoons always seem to make the best of whatever happens, even if Coyote never did trick Raccoon just this way. Raccoons have a knack for accepting change. Adaptability is their key to survival. More willingly than most wildlings, they make do, adjust to new foods, unfamiliar den sites and whatever else is thrust upon them without choice.

But this description of raccoon nature, plus a brief reference to their agile paws, are the only concrete reality in the story. All the action in this tale is the storyteller's fabrication, with Raccoon and Coyote as animals in name only. In action, they are humans, stock characters from slapstick comedy. Practical jokesters each trying to outdo the other in a rivalry that could lead to sequel after sequel at the storytellers' choice.

Listeners would have known from the beginning how the tale would go, and most of them would have been happy to sit back and enjoy every word, absorbing as they went the hint that the raccoon mask and striped tail are samples of nature's basic magic. They are part of nature's most valued gift to the hunted—camouflage to make the wearers all but invisible in the interplay of light and shadow as they wait at forest edge before daring to cross open terrain. Sooner or later some tribal hunters would figure out how this magic works and learn how to copy such markings for their own uses.

Basic camouflage follows two rules. The first calls for imitative coloring of natural surroundings: lions on sundried African grasslands have tawny pelts to match. Raccoons need darker mottled hues to blend with moist forest lands, and since they are not always in forest depths, they need the second basic precept also. Disruptive coloring. A bold contrast of black and white presented in unnatural shapes, fools the hunter so he won't recognize the familiar look of the accustomed prey. This fool-the-eye pattern works especially well when the hunter is at a distance. That straight-line smear of black across raccoon eyes separates the chin from the brow so that actual facial roundness isn't apparent. A hunter's eyes pass over it, not noticing the raccoon.

For added value, the black stripe absorbs the sudden glare of light as the raccoon steps out of the forest into sunny grassland so his eyes aren't dazzled by light and he can see the hunter in time to freeze or flee. And if a predator appears close at hand, the black band hides the black eyes so that the hunter's claws cannot easily make their usual strike intending to blind the hunted.

Nature has given a black eye-mask protection to many species the world around, to those in feathers as well as fur. The raccoon may be the one most often given maskwearer label, but a scanning of any field guide will add many more who earn the name.

When raccoons sleep.
(A BILOXI SIOUX LEGEND)

Two young brothers, neither one yet skilled in hunting, were having an argument. Since neither would yield to the other, they asked their grandfather to settle it.

"Who is right, please?" the older one asked." If we want to catch a raccoon when it is asleep, do we hunt by night or day?"

A ghost of a smile twitched the grandfather's lips as he nodded at the speaker to continue. "And which do you choose?"

The older replied, "I say by night. For I have seen them fishing down by the riverbank in full daylight."

Grandfather turned to the younger lad. "And you?"

"I say by day. I have watched carefully these past three days, morning and evening. Each morning I have seen their footprints in the wet sand—footprints that were not there the evening before. So if they were out walking around by night, they must sleep during the day. And I am sure a raccoon made those prints. Only raccoon prints look like this. . ."

"But I saw them by day," Elder Brother broke in, too upset to remember his manners. "I know I'm right about that!"

Grandfather held up his hand. "You are both right. And you are both wrong. Think again. Could raccoons hunt by either night or day? Many animals see in both dark and daylight, though the raccoon wasn't always as keen-eyed a night-hunter as nowadays. No indeed! Not when the world was young. . ."

The two boys looked at each other, eyes twinkling. Grandfather's voice was slipping into a once-upon-a-time tone and they knew a story was sure to follow if they just kept quiet and listened. So they listened. And this is the tale they heard:

Long, long ago the Most Ancient One of the Raccoons slept at night and hunted by day like all the other Most Ancient Ones. All the others, that is, but Most Ancient Owl who hunted by night. Suddenly Raccoon realized someone else was night hunting. For even if he were up by daybreak, the sand around his best crayfish hole was cluttered with footprints of someone who'd been there ahead of him. The water would be muddied and every fish snug and safe under a rock. Also, if he caught the tangy-sweet scent of ripe persimmons on the air and let his nose lead him to the best breakfast any raccoon could want, he'd find someone else had been there. All the ripe ones were gone. Only hard ones that puckered your mouth were left.

It didn't take Raccoon long to figure out that this somebody was Most Ancient One of the Opossums. Those little splay-toed footprints could belong to no one else. How had such a slowpoke thought of getting up in the dark while everyone else was asleep? Sleeping until daybreak had been the rule since time began, and why would Opossum try to be different?

The only way to answer those questions was to find Opossum and ask. Without thinking further about it, Raccoon followed the footprints and soon caught up with Opossum waddling along as usual.

"Why did you get up before daybreak?" Raccoon demanded.

Opossum blinked his little black eyes and wiggled his pink ears. "Before daybreak?" he repeated, keeping right on going, his long, naked tail making its own track through the dust.

No use asking again. When Opossum didn't want to be bothered, he just flopped down and pretended to be dead as old bones.

Raccoon was standing there, wondering what to do next, when a raspy laugh overhead made him look up.

"Didn't get an answer, did you?" challenged Most Ancient of Jaybirds. "What did you expect? Anybody who can pull that dead-as-bones trick can wiggle out of anything. If you want to know about getting up before daybreak, try it yourself." And off he flew.

Jaybird for once made sense. But Raccoon could go him one better on this getting up before daybreak idea. He would get up in the middle of the night. He would ask Owl to wake him up, just to be sure.

Owl agreed and kept "hoo-hooting" until Raccoon was really awake and on his feet. As it happened, the moon was almost full and he could see quite nicely. In almost no time he was down by the crayfish hole. No footprints. Plenty of crayfish. Raccoon had the best breakfast—or whatever a midnight meal might be *called—he'd had in a long time.*

The next morning, it was Opossum who found footprints and no breakfast. And the morning after that, too. So he began getting up earlier and earlier trying to get ahead of Raccoon, and Raccoon got up earlier still—or stayed up later. Soon they were both hunting by day or night, as the notion took them, eating when they were hungry and sleeping when they needed a rest. So all opossums and raccoons have done ever since, and so they are likely to do forever more, for neither will ever want the other to get ahead of him.

TODAY'S COMMENT

Modern medical research suggests that a raccoon-type split schedule may be the most efficient way to make good use of energy for humans, too. Several small meals at shorter intervals rather than the customary three-a-day may promote better digestion and avoid grogginess that often follows a heavy meal. Also, the body apparently gets more benefit from the first hour or so of sleep than those following. Humans need to know more about sleep needs, of course, as well as ways to work this plan into traditional human schedules. Raccoons already know all they need to know.

Nature's plan of assigning some animals to a daytime shift and others to night duty has long been copied by humans. The motive for rearranging normal procedure thus has usually been to "get ahead" of a competitor just as it was for raccoon and opossum in this old tale.

Although both raccoons and opossums are often cited as strictly nocturnal species, both will come out by day where they feel safe. In coastal areas where tidal ebb and flow regulate the availability of clams, oysters and other seafood, raccoons set their time schedule by the tide instead of the sun and may be seen any hour. The story-teller surely knew this and made hunger the motive for a change in behavior pattern.

Although the legend lets Opossum be first to start the change, Raccoon's wiliness in figuring out his own strategy for success calls for more ingenuity. Science says raccoons will probably always be better at reasoning, for a raccoon brain has six times the capacity of an opossum's. However, the word "opossum," meaning "white faced," came from the same Algonkin language as the word "raccoon" and the two animals are often in the same legends.

OPOSSUM
79

RACOON
22

Drawings: Lumden, 1794.

How raccoons know so much.
(A CADDO TALE)

On a certain long-ago day a Caddo woman stood in a thicket of persimmon trees gazing up into the branches with an angry and bewildered air. Here and there she could see black-masked raccoon faces peering out from the leaves, driblets of yellow persimmon pulp still clinging to their chins, but not a single ripe persimmon remained on any branch or twig. Not one.

"How did they know?" she asked herself, marveling. She and the other village women had been keeping watch faithfully so they would know when the persimmons were ripe. Yesterday they were not ready. Now they were gone. Somehow the raccoons had known just when to come.

She knew—all Caddo knew—that judging the right moment to pick persimmons was tricky. A day, even a half-day, too soon and they were so bitter they puckered your whole mouth. Come too late and they were slush. How did raccoons always know the one right magic moment?

Magic!

She whirled about, heading back to the village. If magic was the answer, the shaman would know.

He did know, of course. And this is the tale he told:

There is a time for each of us to come into this world and a time to leave it. Our Wise Ones have told us that when the Great Spirit calls us to the Hereafter, we must go, take the road west into the unknown as he has commanded. We must go without looking back, without stopping to look around, without taking time to rest weary bones or satisfy hunger. Hunger has no meaning for those on the road west. For it is the soul that makes the journey, not the body. We know this is so. Our Wise Ones have told us time and again. But sometimes someone forgets and then there is a price to pay.

Now it happened that on a certain long-ago day, a man of our tribe was called by the Great Spirit and took the road west as he should. But he had not gone far when a fragrance he knew well and loved, teased his nostrils. Persimmons! Ripe persimmons! He followed his nose and found the tree, the fruit so ripe the yellow pulp was about to push right through the skin. Without even thinking where he was or why, he reached for the nearest one and slurped it down, juice trickling out of both sides of his mouth. He reached for another and as his fingers closed around it he heard a voice and knew it was the Great Spirit who spoke:

"For your disobedience," the voice said, "and for your greed, you will never complete your soul's journey. From this day on you will be animal not human, four-legged and furry forevermore."

The man fell to his knees, pleading forgiveness. He had forgotten where he was, he said, because the persimmons smelled so wonderful. So ripe! How often he had found them only when they were hard and bitter or past eating. But these were at the moment of perfection, and their fragrance wiped all else from his mind.

"O Great Spirit," he went on. "Do you who have given this fruit both bitterness and sweetness, have forgiveness as well as punishment for me?"

The Spirit thought for a moment. "I forgive the greed. But disobedience must be punished. Furry and four-legged you will be. But your feet will still leave human imprint as a reminder of what you have lost. Your hands will keep their human skill at picking this fruit you love and by keen sight and smell and touch you will have first knowledge of its ripeness. In witness of this promise, I now mark you thus. . ."

And with those words the man felt an unseen hand touch his eyes and move on down to his nostrils. He glanced down and saw that he had become a furry animal on four legs, and when he found a brook where he could see his reflection, he saw that his nose was black and shiny, and he had a band of black fur across his cheeks. And he knew that animals with these markings would share the Spirit's promise forever more.

TODAY'S COMMENT

Humans transformed into animals is a theme of folklore in many lands. Sometimes the change is a release from bondage, but more often it is punishment—and a lesson for listeners—as it is here. Raccoons, with their almost-human hands and feet, make believable sinners for this role, and their superb skill at detecting persimmon ripeness gives excuse for leniency.

Persimmons of this puckery kind are native only from the Gulf States to central Pennsylvania and west to Illinois, so such a tale could come only from this area. The persimmons' quick change from bitter to sweet must have seemed magic to the Indians, who could not know that tannin keeps the pulp bitter until it is diluted by frost.

35

Sudden cold softens the fruit, too, and so late-roving raccoons would detect the changes before humans were awake. And that is a bit of nature's trickery well worth its place in Caddo legend. The Caddos, by the way, had another name for this puckery fruit. "Persimmon" skidded into English from the same Algonkin language that gave us "opossum" and "raccoon."

Can a raccoon read peoples' minds?
(A MENOMINI STORY)

The little Menomini village by the lake was astir well before first light. Today they were all going to gather wild rice at the far end of the lake. All, that is, but two old men. These two, once good friends, were now filled with ill-feeling for everyone, especially each other. In their bewilderment and despair at having become blind, each somehow blamed the other for not keeping his eyesight so he could help his blind friend.

They were too wrapped up in their anger to be polite to anyone, let alone helpful, so they had been told to stay behind. Food would be left for them as always and their other needs cared for, too, a granddaughter explained to each, and then the girls hurried off to join the others in the waiting canoes.

Now it happened that an old raccoon had been watching those canoes. And since he thought everyone in the village was gone, he felt he had the village to himself and could poke and pry as he pleased. Once as a young kit he had lived in a village much like this, kept as playmate and pet by a little girl who loved to stroke his fur. But he had grown up and so had she, and she had not tried to find him again when he went off to seek a mate. Now he was curious to learn how much this village was like the one he remembered.

He turned toward the tepees and right away saw something different. A row of poles led from water's edge to a tepee apart from the others, closer to the lake. Something like a vine was looped from one pole to the next, and when he went over to investigate he saw it was strips of sturdy deerskin tied in one of the tightest knots he'd ever touched paw to. He couldn't resist finding out how quickly he could get that knot untied. He managed—but it took more work than he'd expected. So he had to untie the next one, too. And the next and the next until he was reaching for the last one. And just then his nose twitched with a reminder that something good to eat was almost within paw reach.

He looked down and saw two wooden bowls, each filled with the sort of fish stew he had eaten as a kit. One bowl just two steps from the right side of the door flap and the other the same distance to the left. Without stopping to wonder why this food should be there when no villagers remained to eat it, he began to gulp it down, finished up by licking the bowl clean and then moved over to start on the second bowlful.

He was cleaning up the second bowl, when angry voices came from inside the tepee. Voices and thumps and bumps and then he saw a hand come out through the flap. Almost before raccoon could duck behind a tree, two old men came stumbling out, pushing and grabbing at each other, each trying to be first. Now one turned two steps to the right, the other two steps to the left, squatting down and feeling around for the bowl they knew would be waiting.

The moment they touched the bowls and realized they were empty they exploded into a tirade, shouting, yelling, shaking angry fists at each other. It didn't take raccoon long to realize each thought the other had eaten his food. And when they got to their feet, stumbling and fumbling for the deerskin guide rope that now lay on the ground, raccoon suddenly realized the men could not see. They were blind! So that was why the food had been left outside the tent! And why the poles led to the water, the deerskin line waist-high to hang on to.

He had not only eaten their food. He had taken their only way to get a drink of water. And now each was blaming the other for the mischief.

Quietly raccoon slipped down to the bank and began retying the knots, going from post to post, not really knowing what he would do when he was close enough for the blind men to sense his presence.

The man on the right knew first and reached out to grab who-

ever was there—reaching too high, of course, shouting out frightened questions, reaching again and finding nothing to hold on to, tumbling down in a heap with raccoon beneath him.

Raccoon could have squirmed out and been off and away in an instant. But something told him to let the man's hand find a furry paw, and then a shoulder. If the hand would clench to hit or hurt, raccoon was ready to run, but after first contact the hand was gentle. Now it was stroking him nape to tail, feeling the tail's bushy length, then back to the paw with those flexible fingers every Menomini knew.

"Prrrt?" raccoon said in encouraging tone.

"Aispan!" the man cried out, using the Menomini name meaning "handy-paws." And with a happy rush of words and reaching hand he urged the other to feel and learn also.

TODAY'S COMMENT

Raccoons and other animals may or may not read human minds, but they can read human body language—voice tone, gestures, facial expressions, even scents revealing fear or trust. And a raccoon that had once been a pet would not need much by way of a refresher course when next it met a human. In return, animals have their own body language humans may learn. So the story may have been based on an actual incident, with a careful lesson for quarreling humans thrown in.

How to face a wolf.
(A CHEROKEE TALE)

"How do you face a wolf?" the Cherokee storyteller said, not asking anyone in particular, not even those gathered around him at the evening campfire. He was gazing over their heads as if he expected the answer—and his story—to come out of the dusk.

Here and there around the circle a pair of eyes met another and an imperceptible nod passed the message. The story would come. They need only wait and listen.

"If you ask the wolf," the storyteller went on after a pause for his listeners to settle down, "he will tell you he seldom sees another animal's face—just its tail as it runs away. But that is not always true. There was once a certain raccoon...."

He paused again, letting his listeners exchange their grins and nods of approval. When a raccoon was part of a story, they'd find a chuckle or two as well. . .

Raccoon was in his first year of mating and just now taking charge of his own corner of the woods with the best fishing hole up or down the river. And he was so wrapped up in caring for his mates that he forgot to look out for himself.

He was there beside the river one day when all at once a gray shadow beside a low bush turned into a crouching Wolf. He had been too far away to attack Raccoon in one leap, but near enough so that another leap—two at the most—would make it. Luckily, Raccoon was near a big oak tree on the riverbank, and without waiting even to blink at Wolf's yellow-eyed glare he was somer-saulting in a backward midair leap himself.

To Wolf, the tree with its sturdy, widespread branches meant nothing, for he was no climber. But for Raccoon, those branches offered a base for tree-to-tree escape route. One big branch that hung way out over the river even suggested he might try a leap for the far bank, but that was too risky. Halfway up the trunk, Raccoon paused to lift his round black nose, pretending to fix his gaze on someone beyond Wolf's flaring tail as if he had scented even greater danger.

Without thinking, Wolf turned to look, sniff, listen. He had barely flicked one ear when he guessed Raccoon was up to tricks and jerked back, but that was long enough.

"Can't catch me!" Raccoon flung back jauntily as he scram-bled for a higher branch.

Wolf knew Raccoon was right. In his younger days he might have worn himself out leaping at the tree trunk in useless chal-lenge, but he was long past such foolishness. Instead, he'd try a little trickery of his own. Pretend he wasn't really out to catch Raccoon. Just coming to the river for a drink of water—what else? So now with slouching steps he ambled over to the water's edge and began lapping as nonchalantly as if nothing else was on his mind.

In the tree over Wolf's head, Raccoon halted in mid-leap.

What was the big gray fellow up to? Mischief of some sort, Raccoon reminded himself. He inched out onto the big leafy branch stretching over the river—carefully, silently—sure the greenery would hide him as he tried for a better look.

Wolf heard a rustling overhead and glanced up, neck fur bristling. But he saw only the greenery. No hint of black-masked face or furry body. With a shrug he turned back to the water. But the ripples stirred up by his lapping were smoothing out now and suddenly in their very center was that familiar black-eyed, black-cheeked face.

Raccoon's face!

Raccoon had fallen into the river!

The thought flashed through Wolf's mind so fast he was plunging into the river before he knew he'd left the bank, teeth bared to slash.

Instead of fur, there was nothing but water. Water, water, water rushing down his throat, into his nose, into his eyes. Gasping, choking, spitting, Wolf tried to shake himself clear of the threatening flood and make his way back to dry land. Somehow he made it, flung himself down in utter exhaustion, without strength even to open his eyes.

When he did finally get them open, he shut them again as fast as he could. For by then he'd figured out he'd jumped at a reflection. And he knew Raccoon knew and was somewhere right at hand laughing at him. Maybe if he pretended to be asleep Raccoon would go away, take his silly grinning face with him.

Raccoon was grinning but he was not going away. He was just behind the tree scooping up blobs of mud and—WHOP! One blob sealed Wolf's right eye tight shut. WHOP! Another blob sealed the left eye. And those eyes would stay sealed until Wolf could find his way into the river.

Before that could happen, Raccoon intended to be far, far away. And so he was! So he was!

How raccoons catch so many crayfish.
(A TUSCARORA STORY)

On a certain sunny summer day, a small Tuscarora boy and his grandfather were sitting on the bank of a slow-moving creek looking as if they had nothing at all to do. They had been sitting there quite a while, the boy thought, and he didn't see how he could sit still a moment longer. He looked over at his grandfather.

"Eh, grandson?"

"Isn't it time yet?" the boy asked hopefully.

Grandfather squinted up at the sun, pushed out his lower lip to help him think and sucked it back in again.

"So, try and see," he assented, and the boy was down the bank in two leaps.

"Gently!" Grandfather cautioned. "We want to use those bait-sticks again!"

The boy looked back for brief, shame-faced apology and stepped carefully into the water, reaching for each of the three bait sticks in turn and scrambling back up the bank.

"Luck! Luck!" he called out. "Look!"

And it was worth a look, for squirming, claw-waving crayfish were clinging to each piece of venison skewered onto the stick for bait. Quickly the two worked together, prying off the crayfish, tossing them into the basket.

"More bait, now," Grandfather said, starting to reach for the venison strips. "I think. . ."

He stopped, and with a smile handed the stick to the boy. "Your job. Watching is one way to learn. Doing it yourself is better. That's how my grandfather taught me and his his grandfather taught him and. . ."

"And how every other grandfather has done clear back to the first Tuscarora grandfather," the boy finished the familiar words. "Because that is the Tuscarora way."

"Yes, that is our way, grandson." And neither said a word

more until the sticks were baited and their pointed tips pushed down firmly into the creek bed. But when the waiting began again, the puckered frown on the boy's face said plainly that he had a puzzling question.

"So, what is it?" Grandfather asked.

The boy gulped, embarrassed at giving himself away.

"I—well—who taught First Grandfather?" he blurted out. Grandfather threw back his head, chuckling. "Now that is an old question. So I will give you an old answer. My Grandfather told me that First Grandfather thought up the idea all by himself. But your grandmother said he learned how by watching First Raccoon."

"Raccoons make bait-sticks?" the boy asked in amazement.

Grandfather laughed outright. "That's just what I asked! But, no. Raccoons don't have to bother with sticks. They just sit on the edge of the creek and dangle their tails in the water and the crayfish think it's a good place to nap and wriggle right in. Next thing they know, Raccoon flips them up on the bank and into his mouth and those crayfish never have to think about anything again."

"Ai-ee!" the boy whistled, marveling. "But. . ."

"Look!" Grandfather interrupted. "There on the far bank.

Drawing: Lawson, 1709.

Down by that oak. Isn't that a raccoon right now with his tail in the water?"

And it was a raccoon. And maybe his tail was in the creek. Or would be if he moved a bit. But it was just too far away to be sure.

TODAY'S COMMENT

Stories about animals using a dangling tail for fish bait have been told in many lands since ancient times. In Europe, where there were no raccoons, the fox got the credit. In South America it was often the jaguar. Coyote has been the tail dangler in some tales, too. So far, no one has observed any of them in action. But that doesn't say the trick wouldn't work.

Colonial surveyor John Lawson recorded this Tuscarora tale in *A New Voyage to Carolina*, published in London in 1709. He wrote of "crawfish," a common English version of the French *ecrevisse*. "Crawfish" soon changed into "crawdad," incorporating "dad" which was a common diminutive in American frontier folk speech. Raccoons—who do not need a name for them—still feast on these claw-wavers whenever they get a chance, devouring everything except the claws and bits of shell. But first, they make sure with a good solid whack against a rock that their dinner is no longer alive.

The raccoon as trickster.
(AN OJIBWAY VERSION)

Farther north, the Ojibway people, a tribe of Algonkin stock, moved west to Great Lakes country, hoping to find a homeland not yet crowded by white settlements. Their name for the raccoon was "one who picks up things," written by Europeans variably as aisban or espan, among other spellings. And they knew crayfish were one thing raccoons picked up with amazing skill. But instead of giving credit to clever raccoon hands, Ojibway storytellers made raccoon a villain, spinning the tale this way:

Raccoon was a trickster, a smooth talker flattering the naive little crayfish with tales of a marvelous lake just the other side of a nearby hill and then letting them persuade him that they were big and strong enough to help him claim this wonderland for a home they would all share.

Off they all went together, over the hill and down to the lakeshore—where the poor crayfish promptly learned that their share was providing the first meal for a hungry raccoon. Only their claws ever found a home on that storyland shore.

TODAY'S COMMENT

Was the story told to poke fun at certain too-trusting members of the tribe? Was it a warning-in-disguise not to believe white settlers about sharing their homelands and hunting grounds? Many a legend and folk tale had just such a serious message. Of course the raccoon was portrayed as a trickster, a player of impish pranks, in other tales. But here the deception leads to death for those deceived. Yet for tribes that lived by hunting and fishing, death for the hunted meant life for the hunter. So the raccoon would have been seen as a success by the storyteller and his listeners.

As a near-match for this Ojibway tale is one shared by several tribes from areas where opossums and raccoons both feasted on crayfish. This raccoon ne'er-do-well was taunted for being unable to get a full meal of his favorite crayfish treat until he copied the opossum and stretched out on the bank in a play-dead sprawl. The storyteller was hinting, perhaps, that certain young fisherman among his listeners might be more successful if they weren't so fidgety as they waited outside a crayfish burrow.

An ancient artist living on the banks of the Scioto River in Ohio country might have had the same lesson in mind as he carved a raccoon from a chunk of gray stone. His flint knife was sharp, the stone—silica blended with traces of other minerals—was easily shaped when freshly quarried but would harden with exposure to air and heat, so he worked quickly. Soon anyone watching would have recognized the raccoon face with outlined mask, the body

44

crouched on full alert beside a crayfish burrow as one paw probed the opening for the first hint of careless movement within.

Drawing by author of Ohio Mound Builders' stone pipe, 100 B.C.–500 A.D.

The artist's flint knife was sturdy enough to scoop out a hollow midway along the back to serve as a bowl, but he would have needed a well-sharpened sliver of bone or stone to drill the pipestem for the smoke. The pipe platform is 3-1/2 inches long and 1 inch wide, a measurement the artist could have gauged by the length of his fingers. Now all he had to do was add a few slashes for the ringed tail, and smooth it all down with sandstone.

No doubt the owner of the pipe would keep it in a place of honor so that the artist's skill could be seen and admired. And perhaps there would be special nods of approval at the way the bright copper eyes would shine with almost the same glow as real raccoon eyes when caught by torch-fire glare. Three other raccoon figures were among over a hundred effigy pipes unearthed in 1915 by William C. Mills, curator of the Ohio State Archaeological and Historical Society. All of them had been broken as part of the ceremonial burial rites, but most of them could be easily mended. The tally included five species of owls as well as nine other kinds of birds from Great Blue Herons to Bobwhites, Blue Jays and the little birds eventually named as Carolina Paroquets. Fourteen other mammals besides raccoons were pipe figures, too, as well as two kinds of turtles.

Those who have seen them mention the raccoon with its paw in the crayfish hole as one of the best of these trophies from 100 B.C. to 500 A.D. when the Ohio Mound Builder artists were at work. It stirs up thoughts of raccoon fondness for crayfish and gives raccoon patience and skill a firm place among the unwritten records making up North America's earliest history.

Photo: Virginia C. Holmgren

FOUR

WRITTEN RECORDS BEGIN

THE EARLIEST DOCUMENT likely to have some firsthand reference to raccoons has to be the journal Christopher Columbus kept on the first of his four voyages to the American tropics he mistook for The Indies. Certainly the Vikings—and probably other Europeans—made earlier contact with some portion of the New World coastline. But none of them kept written account of where they sailed or what they saw. Although American Indian ancestors left many a reference to raccoons in their oral tales, artifacts and picture-writings, Christopher Columbus was the first historian of the Americas with written records.

Columbus wrote his journals in Spanish, the language of his royal sponsors—Queen Isabella and King Ferdinand—since Spain was his adopted homeland. His voyages stretched over a twelve-year span from the first sailing on August 3, 1492, to the

Postal Stamp: Republic of San Marino.

last homecoming on November 7, 1504. He explored numerous islands from the Bahamas westward to the mainland shores that eventually became Venezuela, as well as along the Isthmus of Panama as far north as

Honduras. His journals contain more than just a mariner's jottings of route, dates, distances, weather, hazards and safe harbors. Columbus also recorded much of the people and their languages and customs, of plant life of every kind, of every animal whether wild or tame—birds, fish, furry quadrupeds and reptiles.

Many plants and animals, especially sea birds, he already knew by name and he added something new of their habits and habitat to his observations. Others he could identify only by some general family likeness. Still others were so different he could scarcely believe he had never seen their like in all his years of voyaging across the Mediterranean, south to Africa, north to England and Iceland. Nor were they mentioned in Pliny's famous Latin text on animals or in Marco Polo's account of those fabulous Asian Indies or in any other book of travels current in Europe.

Each night as he took pen in hand to tell of the day's discoveries he made special effort to describe what was familiar as well as all that was strange. So his journals became a detailed compilation of seamanship, geography, human history and natural history all in one—a remarkable introduction to lands never before on written record as well as to one small furry animal with a mask-like face pattern.

Columbus and his crews were bound to meet the mask wearer early in their voyaging, for raccoons were native then to almost all the islands explored on the first two of their four expeditions. (One island is still named Raccoon Cay.) So we begin with the first landing on American shores, October 12, 1492, and we keep looking as we read for some mention of those raccoon identification marks—masked face, ringed tail, handlike paws. Pass over the Admiral's pleasure at finding so many parrots. The big-beaked birds had been imported to Europe from both Asia and Africa for centuries, but Columbus gave them special mention—and collected cages of them to take back as souvenirs—because most Europeans believed that parrots lived only in lands rich in gold. Pass over his amazement at a lizard of prodigious size and unknown name soon to be called by the Taino Indian word *iguana*. We keep on reading.

By now it is October 17 and the *Santa María, Niña* and *Pinta* are ready for a two-day anchorage at the northern tip of a longish island with friendly fisherfolk and pleasant greenery. Columbus named it Fernandina, to honor the king, but it is now Long Island. Neither name holds a hint of a better choice. But it could rightfully be re-named Raccoon Island, because right here is where Columbus saw two shaggy-furred pets playing near a fisherman's hut with rough-and tumble, jump-and-sprawl exuberance. He watched their antics awhile, remembering dogs he'd seen at play as a boy in Genoa.

He must have thought they were dogs, for that is what he called them in his journal. *Perros*, he wrote in his careful Spanish script. And then he must have paused, searching for the right word to explain that these two weren't exactly like any dogs he'd seen elsewhere. Of course dogs come in many sizes, colors, length of coat and sharpness of muzzle. Even taking all that into consideration, these two were different.

One marking especially had caught his eye, reminding him of carnival clowns he'd seen somewhere with faces painted in black and white—soot and whitewash—for slapdash disguise. These two had similar smears across the eyes. So he gave them a clown's name, *perro mastin*, "clownlike dog."

He wrote the new-coined phrase with a satisfied flourish, unaware that he had given the American raccoon its first entry on written record, its first name in a European language.

As it turned out, Columbus himself would give raccoons a second label very shortly, and some of his crew would add a third. Within the next two weeks he realized that these island Indians had two kinds of dogs: shaggy-coated "clowns" and others with shorter fur, all one color or spotted in black and white or brown like street mongrels back in Spain. Neither kind ever barked—an amazing trait for dogs of any kind or color—and the Admiral mentioned it in his journal: *Perros que son mudos en que no ladraban.* "Dogs that are mute in that they do not bark." A careful wording. But his companions and future Spanish settlers shortened it to *perro mudo,* as if the animals were mute. Everybody who came to the Indies soon learned that *mudos* could whimper, whine, growl, yelp. But they never gave out with an honest, dog-ish bark and so the misnomer was kept in circulation for both village dogs and raccoons. After all, both looked like dogs. Both were kept as pets by the Indians and both were often used as food.

When Columbus and his crews anchored off Cuba's northeast shores in early November, some of the sailors returned from exploring with word they'd seen an animal like a badger, *tejón* in Spanish.

Because this turned out to be the same animal as the Admiral's *perro mastin,* an inlet still marked Bahía de Perros on today's maps may be the very spot where "badgerlike dog," *perro tejón,* became a raccoon alias, replacing the clownlike label few understood. At any rate, for more than a century perro tejón, a combination of two wrongs made, another misnomer for the raccoon.

Historians who honor Columbus are prone to insist that the Admiral knew a dog when he saw one and would never have given the raccoon such a label. But he did not know a raccoon when he saw one! Neither did any other European. And they can be excused for this error just as others can be excused for confusing the raccoon with the wild cat. One was misled by the ringed tail, the other by the raccoon's doglike behavior. The science of identifying new species was not sophisticated enough at the time to allow observers to make the sort of judgment any high school biology student should be able to make today. Many more Europeans would make similar errors before the raccoon achieved the scientific status to which it is entitled.

Columbus's writings show he differentiated between dogs of two different kinds: when he meant the village dogs or the Indies pets, his term was *perro mudo*. When he meant the raccoon, he wrote of the *perro mastin* and told how it lived almost exclusively on fish. He learned of their fishing skill on his second voyage while at anchor off Cuba's south shore May 22, 1494. Also on the second voyage, one of his companions—the gentleman adventurer Guillermo Coma of Aragón—would explain that these fish-catching dogs could neither bark "nor wag the tail." That lack of a tail wag—added to the fishing skill and lack of bark—should have certified the *perro mastin* as something special. But Coma's comment was in a letter to his old professor—Niccolò Scillacio (or Syllacio) of Pavia—who rushed it into Latin for publication unaware he had misread Coma's "ni rabean" (nor wag the tail) for "ni rabian" (nor go mad). Presence or absence of the dot for an "*i*" can be disputed. But Coma could not possibly have learned enough Taino in those few weeks to discuss rabies. Noticing the lack of a tail-wag took only a brief glance. Unfortunately, no scholar has reported this misreading, probably because all attention has gone to citing this letter as the first time the spelling "Columbus" appeared in print.

In Spain, however, several who saw these odd Indies dogs wrote of them as "malformed," in other words visibly different from European dogs. And back in the Indies, those who stayed after the second and third voyages reported that the little short-coated village dogs soon recovered their ability to bark by hearing newly-arrived Spanish dogs sound off vociferously, so their silence had been a matter of training. But the shaggy *mastines* never did learn to bark, no matter how faithfully some Spaniard tried to teach them.

Final proof of raccoon identity and dog alias is in a

1570s study of Mexican animals by the famous Spanish physician-naturalist Francisco Hernández. Badgerdog, he wrote in Latin, was the name most often used by Spaniards in the New World for the uniquely American animal known to Aztec Indians as *mapachitli*. "One who takes everything in its hands" is the translation of this tongue-twister—a perfect match for raccoon behavior—and Hernández urged his fellow Spaniards to use it instead of their own erroneous label. The Spaniards did so eventually—softening it to the less gutteral *mapache*.

The raccoon, however, would continue to acquire all sorts of guess-again names that didn't fit. The confusion might have been cleared up far earlier if the Spanish monarchs had allowed the writings of Columbus and other explorers to be published. But most of them were banned to prevent rival nations from learning of the wonders of the New World. Columbus' journals were not published until 1571—and then only in an Italian translation of a copy, for the originals turned over to the monarchs had vanished. The remarkable study by Hernández was burned in a palace fire, but copies survived and a Spanish edition of his Latin text was published in 1615. The Latin was published later in 1635. Several other early accounts did not get into print until the nineteenth century, but they are available now in Spanish—government-sponsored editions that give us a viewpoint even people of the time did not always have—and provide a few more oldtime aliases for the raccoon.

The raccoon's bushy tail was bound to suggest a fox to Europeans. In the 1520s some adventurous Spaniards sailed north past Florida and stopped to explore offshore islands (Parris Island, Hilton Head and their neighbors) and returned to tell the learned official Indies historian—Gonzalo Fernández de Oviedo—they had seen foxlike animals with faces "*muy pintada*." Translated as "painted faces," this indicates their fox was a raccoon, the first reported in an area now part of the United States.

First the Spanish and then the French would try to establish colonies on these sea islands. Both would abandon the effort, but when the French leader, Jean Ribaut, gathered a second band in 1564, he included the artist Jacques LeMoyne de Margues to depict this land holding wonders "that could not with tongue be expressed." Luckily LeMoyne's water colors survived as engravings, and were first published in the 1590s and then reprinted many times since. One shows what may be a raccoon sizzling over an island Indian cookfire and others portray raccoon tails displayed on Indian belts and headdresses farther south along the present St. John's River in Florida.

"Foxlike" would also be the label for raccoon used by 13-year-old Hernando de Escalante Fontaneda of the Spanish colony at Cartagena. In 1552, while en route to Spain for further schooling, he was shipwrecked on the Florida Keys and spent the next seventeen years with an Indian tribe. Finally rescued by Spaniards, he went on to Spain and wrote his memoirs, mentioning he had come to know "a certain animal that looks like a fox yet is not, but a different thing from it. It is fat and good to eat."

Many years later archaeologists on the Bahama island of Eleuthera unearthed wooden stools carved in animal shapes by ancient Taino Indians of the tribe that first welcomed Columbus. "Foxlike" was the museum curator's identification of the animal portrayed. But Columbus saw similar stools on Cuba in 1492 and when he returned on his second voyage with more knowledge of the Taino tongue he learned that these animals had an almost magical skill in slipping out of their cord bindings and escaping to nearby lakes to frolic in the moonlight—a tale that more than hints the models were raccoons.

Oviedo himself would compare raccoons to foxes—and dogs, monkeys, and even clowns—when he wrote of his own experiences with these unfamiliar animals:

"There are some small animals like little grizzled dogs and their snout and the forelegs and the feet are black, and they are almost of the same likeness as the foxes of Spain—and they are not less wily and given to biting. But also they are tamed for pets and are very clownish and amusing, almost like monkeys, and their principal food—that which they like best to eat—are crabs, on which they are thought largely to subsist. I had one of them that a ship brought me from the coast of Cartagena, which they said the Indian hunters had traded for two fish hooks, and I had it for along time, fastened to a chain. And these animals are very playful and not dirty like monkeys. "

Anyone who knows raccoons can immediately identify these doglike, foxlike, monkeylike animals. Anyone who doesn't is likely to accept the dog tag with no more than a shrug. At least that's how it worked in the 16th century. Even the Tupi name for raccoons—*aguara-po-pay*, "leaper upon crabs and crayfish"—was turned into "crab-catching dog" by most Europeans. *Perro cangrejero* in Spanish and *chien crabier* in French were commonly used.

However, German miners in Venezuela in the 1530s (sent by the Welser banking house of Augsburg to collect at firsthand a debt owed by Spanish King Carlos) made a better choice. They saw a furry animal patting and dunking its catch at streamside and were reminded of a fish-seller scraping off scales to please a waiting customer.

"*Schupp!*" one of them must have said, nudging his neighbor to share the joke of an animal playing fish vendor. It was the word for fish scales, or one who scraped them off, or even for whoever sold fish or caught them.

Someone in the group now thought of taking *schupp* pelts back to show furriers—a new trade item. Since South American raccoons have thinner fur to match the warmer weather, a boom in raccoon fur trade didn't come until later when northern pelts were available. But when the first northern furs arrived in Germany, the term *schupp* was waiting. From Germany it spread to every nearby country where fur hats were a winter necessity, undergoing whatever change in spelling fit the local language. Consequently, the Swedish *sjupp*, Finnish *siupp*, Dutch *schob*, Danish *skjob*, Polish *szop* and Russian *jenot* were on trading lists well into the 19th century.

Schupp was also the name furriers gave a North American marten, now officially identified as *Martes pennanti*, whose fur was similar in thickness to that of raccoons but who lacked the markings. Europeans dyed both pelts to match black bears and passed them off as bearskin—scarce in Europe for making the huge hive-shaped military hats made popular by the dashing 17th-century Hungarian Hussars. Oddly, only the marten keeps its "fisher" name on the North American mammal lists although it neither catches fish nor eats them except in extreme hunger. The misnomer has been cited time and again as an unsolved riddle since few modern naturalists ever heard of the furriers' marten-for-raccoon-for-bear switch of olden days. Meanwhile any French Canadians who had called the raccoon *chat sauvage* were soon calling the marten *chat sauvage noir*. Audubon was among several 19th-century naturalists who listed both "fisher" and "black cat" as aliases for the species they identified as Pennant's marten, and this sharing of aliases makes another link in the cat-for-coon confusion in earliest pioneer days.

The first published portrait of a raccoon would have a still different title. It appeared in 1551 in one of the most famous books of the century—*Historia Animalium* by Conrad Gesner of Zurich, respected physician, naturalist and scholar. He set out to record everything of importance written about every four-legged animal known since the time of Aristotle. He consulted numerous authorities (but not Augsburg furriers apparently) and so could include New World species he had never seen.

Among these the raccoon appeared both as "a dog called fisher" and as "malformed dogs" although Gesner did not have any idea these were the same animal as the one portrayed in a sketch shown him by a fellow physician-naturalist, Pierre Belon of Paris, who headed the museum of natural history at the *Collège de France*. Belon himself knew nothing of this animal except that it came from the Caribbean Indies and had been accompanied by a smaller animal, also unknown in Europe. They could see by the sketch that this larger one had been a pet, since it wore a collar, but no written account added further the clarification.

From *Historia Animalium*, Conrad Gesner, 1551.

Gesner might have ignored these two Indies odditities for want of further details. But the renowned physician-naturalist Antonio Brasavolus (physician to three French kings and four popes) gave him a sketch and insisted he use it. He also insisted both unknown animals be identified by a group label, for want of specific name. Brasavolus was a fanatic on group classification, urging a return to Aristotle's system. The Greeks had grouped animals by appearance and actions, but most writers since then had listed their entries in alphabetical order, doing little classifying beyond separating domestic species from wild ones. Gesner himself followed the alphabet, but he yielded to his consultant's demand that these two be enrolled in a group identified by the Latin word *mus*, a term used by some only for mice and rats but originally including sable, ermine, marten—almost any furry species with a pointed snout. Gesner began with the smaller animal, labeling it *Indicus mus* and the larger one *Mus Indicus alius*, "another Indies rodent," and comparing both to the Egyptian mongoose. Perhaps Gesner, like most Europeans then, was a bit vague about the geographical distance between Columbus' Indies and the old India. Or perhaps he just thought one odd-looking foreign species deserved another.

Gesner did allow himself to mention that the animal pictured had a bushy tail like a wild cat's, not the thinner one of a rat, mongoose, or weasel. Most readers ignored this faint protest and thought the animal was a rat, especially since Marco Polo's writings had prepared them to expect Indies rats of gigantic size.

Edward Topsell, however, who translated Gesner's book to English, stuck with the phonetic translation of *mus* as "mouse." Readers who matched the picture with the raccoon, however, promoted it to rat. Its smaller companion was eventually identified as a Jamaican rat until the Taino Indian name of *hutia*—used by Columbus when he caged one or two as companion souvenirs for the *perros mastines*—was once again established.

Columbus brought back raccoons and *hutias* on both his first and second voyages. Those on the first stormy homebound passage were seen in Lisbon, when Columbus was forced to stop there for repairs, although they apparently did not survive long after reaching Spain. But there are too many references to those brought on the second voyage to doubt their presence. Columbus even mentioned he took them aboard at his last stop for supplies on the island he named Guadalupe (now French Guadaloupe). Raccoons still abound there and one is pictured on a forty centime postage stamp of 1973 gazing from a tree-branch perch with the same faraway look that a mother raccoon might have had as she watched the ships—with her kits aboard—vanish over the horizon in the summer of 1496.

In Spain, Andres Bernaldez wrote of seeing these two—*ratones grandissimos* called *hutias* by the Indians and the dogs of medium

Guadalupe postal stamp, 1973.

size that did not bark and lived mostly on fish, yet when fattened for the table had the *buen sabor* of roast kid. Bernaldez did not admit he had eaten dog, but declared several others at court had done so, and over the following years the likeness to kid would be mentioned many times by Spaniards while the English usually said raccoon tasted like lamb.

Certainly the hundreds of hopeful Spaniards who came to the Caribbean on the second voyage with greedy dreams of gold had plenty of chances to know the taste of raccoon meat, for it became their staple food—as long as the raccoons lasted. Tame ones in Indian villages were the first to go, and the wild ones were quickly hunted down by the hounds the Spaniards had brought with them—huge beasts, twice the size of any raccoon. In 1513 when settlers asked the historian Oviedo what happened to the "non-barkers," he told them straight out they'd been eaten into extinction. On an island, once gone is gone forever since no other animals are nearby to move in for replacement.

First to vanish were the raccoons on the island Columbus had made his headquarters and named Española. European publishers Latinized this name to Hispaniola—a name that has survived—and it is still used to describe the island containing Haiti and the Dominican Republic. Raccoons on Cuba and Jamaica lasted somewhat longer, since Spanish settlers did not arrive so early or in such great numbers. The mask wearers hid out in the hills by day, slipping down to raid gardens and sugar cane fields at night with such stealth that the damage was often blamed on ghosts. In 1687 British physician-naturalist Sir

Hans Sloane wrote of seeing raccoons on Jamaica where they had long been thought extinct, but his report was the last sighting. Meanwhile, Oviedo's readers knew he'd rejoiced to find non-barking fisher-dogs in Nicaragua and elsewhere—enough to guarantee there would always be plenty for others to see and enjoy as pets. If anyone had told him that these affectionate, impish animals would get their first official listing as *mus indicus*, "Indies rats," he would have been highly indignant.

Probably that estimable scholar, Conrad Gesner of Zurich, never learned that his outsize *mus* would be so popular a pet or be known to so many as a raccoon. His own reputation, however, was assured, for his first volume on quadrupeds was followed by a second on fish and a third on birds to complete his *Historia Animalium*. The three volumes became the supreme authority on animal life for European scholars for the next two hundred years and misled many a reader who had turned to it to set them straight on the American animal with the ringed tail. Even when the raccoon was well known, some who spoke of it—the English sea captain William Dampier for one—would think it necessary to add that it was a kind of rat.

First to publish the Indian name "raccoon" was red-haired, undauntable Captain John Smith who published a *True Relation* of life in Virginia's Jamestown Colony in 1608. He'd heard the name spoken by Algonkin chief Powhatan and his daughter Pocahontas. Trying to match letters to sound, *rahaughcums* was his first written attempt, followed by *arocouns*, *rarowcuns* and a few other versions as he told how Powhatan covered his chieftain's platform with the thick-furred pelts, the tails hanging down all around in display. Alive, he added, this furry one was much like a badger, except that it lived in trees like a squirrel. The London artist who illustrated this volume must not have seen the raccoon pelts, for he pictured Powhatan on a bare platform—no sign of fur padding or ring-tailed fringe—in one scene, and seated on a plain strip of cloth in another. The latter shows Smith a prisoner with

Pocahontas asking her father to spare his life, a story Smith was proud to tell and re-tell.

From Smith's *Generall Historie*, 1624.

Ten years later colonist William Wood of New England gave his readers more details about this American animal that could now also be seen in the zoo at the Tower of London:

"The Rackoone is a deep-furred beast, not much unlikebadger, having a tayle like a Fox, as good meat as a Lambe. . . These beasts in the daytime sleep in hollow trees; in the moonshine night they goe to feed on clammes at a low tide by the Sea-side where the English hunt them with their dogges."

A few years later another New Englander—John Josselyn— informed his readers that in London the spelling was "rattoon," and this variant was common from 1656 to 1750. Was Gesner's *mus* to blame? Or had one influential writer misheard the central consonant and others followed suit? Evidently the sound of *"t"* can be misunderstood for *"c"* or *"k"*—especially in a foreign word. For instance, the word certain Italians and Spaniards (including Columbus) knew as *mastin* came from Arabic *maskhara* and became "mask" or "maskwearer" in most European languages. But in *mastin* and *mastiff* (naming a dog with masklike black muzzle) the *"t"* sound came through as it might have done in "rattoon."

In the 1730s Nathaniel Bailey's English dictionary listed "raccoon" as an animal from New England and "rattoon" as an inhabitant of the West Indies. Esteemed lexicographer Samuel Johnson was so sure this was correct that he kept the two entries through eight editions of his famous tome:

> *"rackoon*: The rackoon is a new England animal like a badger, having a tail like a fox, being cloathedwith a thick and deep furr: it sleeps in the daytime in a hollow tree and goes out a-nights when the moon shines, to feed on the sea-side, where it is hunted by dogs. *rattoon*: A West India fox which has this peculiar property, that if anything be offered it that has lain in water, it will wipe it and turn it around with its forepaws before it will put it in its mouth."

In spite of the confusion, his "rattoon" is obviously the same species as his New England "rackoon." And Johnson's reputation as an authority would keep the misspelling in circulation for quite a time.

The most important writer to be led astray by Gesner and Samuel Johnson was the French naturalist Buffon. His *Histoire Naturelle* would outsell all similar works in the 18th century, so his influence was far-reaching. He accepted *mus* and *rattoon* as the correct categorization, and therefore enrolled the mask-wear-er in his book at *raton*, "little rat." As it happened, *raton* is also French slang for anyone of baby-faced cuteness, and Buffon soon learned that baby raccoons can be appeal-ingly cute. He never used this as an alibi for his *raton* classi-fication, however, probably because the choice was only one of the many ways he

Buffon, Naturalist's Library,1829.

defied his arch rival, Linneaeus of Sweden, who had assigned raccoons to a very different category. The Buffon-Linnaeus feud amused most of their con-temporaries, but the two involved were deadly seri-ous and so raccoon classifi-cation got a bit more atten-tion than it might other-wise have rated.

Linnaeus, Swainson, 1835.

FIVE

SO IT'S A RACCOON—BUT WHAT'S THAT?

IN 1747 CROWN PRINCE FREDRIK of Sweden gave Carl Linnaeus—naturalist, author, professor at Uppsala University—a new furry animal for his private zoo. Neither prince nor professor had seen a live animal of this sort before. It was known in Sweden only for its fur and by the fur-trade name *sjupp*. Now Linnaeus was asked to learn its ways and publish a full account.

Eagerly he set to work, and readers of the *Proceedings* of the Swedish Royal Academy of Sciences must have been delighted with his story of a wild animal from a land half a world away that had become used to people, let children stroke his fur (but never, never pick him up!) and considered raisins, almonds, sugar cubes and fresh fruit his favorite food. His sense of smell was so acute that he could instantly detect where such treats were hidden and boldly pawed at pocket, cupboard, bag, box or any other hiding place until he got what he wanted. He could pass the time happily playing patty-cake with any small object that took his fancy, often dunking it into his water bowl with both agile paws.

Unfortunately, those paws were also able to unlatch his cage door, and one night he set himself free, climbed over the backyard fence into a neighbor's yard and was killed by an alert watch dog. Linnaeus grieved at this loss, but he was too much the scientist not to realize that he could dissect the body and learn much of *sjupp* anatomy.

Linnaeus was confident in his ability to assign this species to its proper place among the other four-legged forest hunters in his system of classifying nature's gifts—plants, animals, minerals—that had become his chief work. Similar foot structure was one criterion for placing species in the same group. Similarity of teeth and jaws was another. On both counts, as well as others, he observed that the *sjupp* resembled the bears, especially in their habit of walking with feet fully flat on the ground, leaving an entire paw print. Therefore *sjupp* was set down as a member of the *Genus Ursus*, Latin for "of the bearkind."

Genus, by Linnaean definition, implied a broader group than in modern classification and was comparable to the current use of *Family*—a term Linnaeus did not employ. His system called for following each generic label with a description of features others in the genus did not share. His first choice for the *sjupp* was *cauda elongata*, "long-tailed." But he'd used this same phrase for the wolverine and he had not yet heard of the word "raccoon" in any spelling and so he changed the label to *Ursus cauda annulata, fascia per oculos transversi*—"ring-tailed bear with transverse bands through the eyes."

He now considered his classification of *sjupp* completed and turned to more pressing duties. His days were crowded with work on new editions of his *Systema Naturae*, lectures at the university, personal conferences with students and colleagues, and frequent field trips. He insisted on field work, on learning from nature itself as well as from books, both as a principle for his students and for himself. Unexpectedly he also discovered he had more to learn about the *sjupp*.

In 1748 he recommended one of his favorite students, a young Finn named Pehr Kalm, for a scholarship to study North American plants and animals in a tour of English, Dutch and Swedish seaboard colonies. Now Kalm was back with the surprising news that in all English colonies the name for *sjupp* was "raccoon"—a word taken from some Indian language. He'd heard other Indian names, too, since each tribe had its own language, but "raccoon" was the name in most common usage.

Kalm added that the raccoon's oddly curved penis bone—which Linnaeus had noticed when dissecting his pet—was hailed by the Indians as the perfect tool for cleaning their tobacco pipes. The colonists considered raccoons related to bears also, "because both leap with all four feet at once," unaware Tupi Indians had made the same observation. Thick raccoon fur was prized for warm caps, with the tail still attached so that it could be wrapped around the neck like a scarf. European furriers valued it also and raccoon pelts were rated next to beaver as trade goods. "The skin is sold for eighteen pence at Philadelphia," Kalm wrote in his journal on February 8, 1749. He also noted that raccoons had been known to den up during a snowstorm for a whole week, living without food "by sucking and licking its paws."

Actually, raccoons survive such ordeals by living off their stored fat, which they gain in good supply through steady over-eating in late autumn. But if Kalm missed this facet of raccoon behavior, he did learn that they eat almost everything they get their paws on—fish and fowl and small animals as well as fruit and newly ripe corn. To illustrate this varied menu the title page for the Dutch edition

From *Travels in North America* (Dutch edition, 1772), Pehr Kalm.

of his *Travels in North America* showed a plump raccoon with a chipmunk at one side and watermelons at the other.

Raccoons were often taken as pets by the colonists, and soon developed a craving for sweets, helping themselves to whatever was not under lock and key. Kalm had seen one plunging both paws into a molasses jug and licking off every drop, going back for more. "The women therefore have everyday some complaint," Kalm summed up the situation, adding that complaints were justified because raccoons also raided the chicken coops on occasion. But raccoons continued to be adopted as pets and seemed to be truly fond of their owners even if they never relinquished their raccoon rights to take whatever they wanted to eat.

RACOON.

From *Travels in North America*, Pehr Kalm.

Linnaeus would credit Kalm as source for adding "raccoon" to several other aliases on his list, including Gesner's *mus*, of course, and the *Vulipi affinis americana*, "American relative of the fox," of English naturalist John Ray, and the ring-tailed water dabbler in Albert Seba's Amsterdam museum enrolled as *Felis americana montana*,

"American mountain cat." By 1758 Linnaeus' tenth edition of *Systema Naturae* had an important revision—probably the most important step in classification yet made—he limited all Latin nomenclature to just two terms, one to name the genus and a second to identify the species.

Linnaeus begged all other classifiers to accept these binomials for their own publications, thereby granting science the boon of a terminology both brief and universal—easily learned and remembered and the same worldwide in a language all scholars understood. Some writers agreed at once. Others never did, including Buffon. Worldwide acceptance did not come officially until one international meeting of zoologists in 1889 and another in 1905 worked out initial rules of acceptance. Disagreements continue even now, and a system for revising binomials with approval of official committees has been in effect for some time. Many such revisions retain the specific name, correcting only a genus chosen in earlier days when similarities were more difficult to determine, and *Ursus lotor* "washer bear"—the new Linnean binomial—was one of the first to be rejected. Linnaeus had thought it one of his best—as did many others—and he did not live to know of its ultimate rejection.

Oddly, even while Linnaeus' Latin binomial was being erased from official texts, the phrase "washer-bear" was being translated into everyday languages all over Europe. It replaced many of the furriers' *schupp-sjupp* labels on zoo cages, especially in Sweden and Germany. Swedish *tvättbjörn* and German *waschbär* are still used far more often than "raccoon" or even a more phonetic "rakun." And even in North America many newspaper and magazine writers still name the raccoon a "little brother of the bear," unaware that *lotor* was officially removed from *Ursus* category in 1780.

A German physician and professor of natural history—Gottlieb Conrad Christian Storr—presented the full description of raccoon anatomy to prove it was neither bear, rat, dog nor any other Old World genus, but distinctly *sui generis*, of its own kind. The ghost of a long-dead colleague, the 16th-century Spaniard Francisco Hernández, would have nodded approval, for he had used that very phrase in 1575. He might also have understood why Storr chose *Procyon* as the new-coined genus label, for Hernández had reported that most Spaniards of his day had considered the raccoon a kind of dog, and *cyon* is Latinized Greek for "dog." The prefix *pro*, however, has seventeen different translations in a desk-size Latin-English dictionary, including "before, for, in favor of, in front of, instead of, as, just as, like," etc. Since Storr did not explain which he had in mind, interpretation has been reader's choice. Because astronomers of a century earlier had used *Procyon* for a newly discovered star which appears in the heavens shortly before the Dog Star, Sirius, many classifiers have assumed that Storr chose also "before the dog" as the meaning.

But no one in that era would have thought that the raccoon—a New World species—had been created before the dog, named in some of the oldest writings of the Old World. It is possible Storr knew raccoons often had to flee *in front of* dogs when a coon hunt was underway. But it is even more likely that he was thinking of "like a dog." Almost certainly he knew Hernández said the common name among Spaniards was "badgerlike dog." He may even have known that Columbus wrote of *perro mastin* and *perro mudo*. Beyond doubt Storr knew that three of his contemporaries—Linnaeus, Buffon in Paris, Jacob Klein in Lübeck—had noted doglike ways in their pet raccoons. Pehr Kalm, returning from America, had said pet raccoons "ran about the streets like a domestic animal." And William Byrd of Virginia, writing of his experiences while establishing the dividing line between Virginia and North Carolina in 1728 plainly thought of the raccoon as doglike for his description reads:

". . .a Raccoon, which is of the Dogkind, and as big as a small Fox, tho' its Legs are Shorter, and when fat has a much higher relish than Mutton or Kid. . . very fond of Indian corn and Parsimons."

Whatever Storr had in mind, modern classifiers have backed him in "like a dog" rating, for when all the Order Carnivora is divided into two superfamilies—one for species of doglike ways and the other for those of more catlike nature—the raccoon is placed with the Canoidea along with true dogs, wolves, foxes, bears, weasels, martens and their kin. Therefore it seems correct to translate as "doglike washer" Storr's label of *Procyon lotor*, the binomial the raccoon still wears today and probably always will, for science does not permit change of these two-word titles without convincing reason.

In Paris, meanwhile, Buffon was thoroughly enjoying his pet raccoons and preparing a study that would clearly outdo the one Linnaeus had published. He was lucky to have a female with kits and to have the mother with him in the natural history museum for over a year, so he had far more time than his rival to learn raccoon ways. The result would be a fascinating addition to the popular volume on quadrupeds of his *Histoire Naturelle*, and like all his work it was in French, since being anti-Latin was part of his war against Linnaeus. Buffon also chose different categories, enrolling his *raton* in *Order Carnassiers* and *Family Carnivores*, both terms meaning "flesh-eaters," and thence in *Tribu Plantigrade*, "flatfooted" and *Genre Raton*. A few years before his death he was forced by royal command to make the official name *raton laveur* "washer rat" to conform in part with the Linnaean label that had become so popular.

So Buffon lost on one point of nomenclature but made up for it with breadth of coverage, mentioning among other discoveries that raccoons retire to a private toilet place if their quarters provide room for such cleanliness.

He also discussed in detail the washing action that caught every raccoon-watcher's attention. Moist, juicy foods—meat or fruit—were almost never put in the water bowl, he noted, but anything dry and hard—such as bread crusts—went in straightaway unless the animal was extremely hungry. He suggested, therefore, that raccoons might not have a sufficient supply of saliva. The arguments on this matter continue to the present and one recent theory is that immersion in water intensifies the sensitivity of the raccoons paws and therefore its ability to identify what is handled and to store that knowledge for future use. As for saliva sufficiency, dry hard foods are not on the raccoons' natural menu, and today's veterinarians say they have enough saliva for normal needs.

Buffon also outscored Linnaeus in presenting the South American Raccoon as a different species, thanks to his friend in the French colony of Cayenne, one Monsieur de la Borde. A crate containing this gift was shipped from Cayenne June 12, 1774, and when Buffon read the label he exploded in exasperation. Because his friend called it a dog: *chien crabier*, "crab-eating dog."

Evidently Buffon had not heard—or had forgotten—that raccoons had worn "doglike" label in the Caribbean since 1492. At any rate, he would not allow them to keep such a misnomer. "Since we are ignorant of its real name," he wrote, "we will call it *Raton Crabier*." And that is still its name in French, while the Latin label follows suit with *Procyon cancrivorus*. The shared genus marks it as the closest relative of *Procyon lotor*, while the different species classifications grant each its own individuality even though the North American Raccoon likes crabs every bit as much as the southerner—and the "crab-eater" is as much a "washer," a dabbler in water, as the *Lotor*.

These two share the Family Procyonidae with four relatives each in a different genus—coati, cacomistle, kinkajou and olingo—which are also native only to the Americas.

They are described in Chapter Ten along with two Old World species that may or may not warrant Procyonid classification—the Red Panda and its popular giant-sized cousin—both from those lands of Old India known to Marco Polo.

Photo: John Pitman

SIX

RACCOONS ON THE AMERICAN FRONTIER—AND BEYOND

IN THE SAME DECADE that raccoons were given full status as a species "of its own kind," independent of dogs, rats, bears or any other Old World genus, Britain's thirteen North American colonies won their independence, too, and emerged as the United States of America. And because raccoons had already become closely interwoven with American life, their pelts had a small part in the battle for freedom not usually mentioned in history books.

Money for financing the Revolution was always difficult to find, especially when it came to providing warm winter uniforms. When men of the New Jersey militia found themselves in danger of suffering from frost-bitten ears, they solved the problem by sending home for those tried and trusty ear-warmers, coonskin caps. A whole company of fur-capped marchers with ringed tails flaunted in dangling display usually brought a laughing sally from watchers, along with a few salty jibes about New Jersey being so short of real men they had to enlist raccoons instead.

"Oh, you Raccoons!" came the teasing call time and again. And the cap-wearers grinned in answer, patting their warm ear and accepting the nickname with aplomb. When they were finally  mustered out the official report read: "Each devoted Raccoon to receive down forty soft or paper dollars."

Money, soft paper or hard coin, was scarce after the war, and officers as well as men were eager to claim the free land along the Ohio River they'd been promised when victory was secure. When the soldiers-turned-settlers finally reached Ohio country they found raccoons were already there in good number.

Even settlers who had been city bred knew that raccoon fur would provide caps, coats, cushions, bed covers. Some of them also knew its flesh had been considered good meat—at least better than no meat at all and easier to get than deer. Oldtimers assured them raccoons could be roasted whole with stuffing or split in half and cooked over an open fire on the trail, even cut in strips of fatty sidemeat and smoked like bacon.

"Don't forget to save the fat," someone was sure to warn. "Nothing better for healing sprains and bruises, softening leather or using in recipes instead of lard. Can't do without it."

Doing without, the new settlers learned, was the way of life on the frontier for almost everything except raccoons. And it was not just their meat and fur that were valued, but the animals' natural instincts as well. For one thing, if you were on unknown ground that looked more than a little soggy, you could avoid stepping into quagmire or quicksand if you could follow raccoon tracks, for those babylike footprints always marked safe ground. Also, if you wanted to cross a river without having to wade or swim, look for raccoon tracks again. They might lead you along the bank to where some storm-felled tree reached shore to shore for a "raccoon bridge." If you dared, you could cross upright on two feet, but it was usually safer to follow the raccoon's lead and go on all fours. Even then you might have trouble. A raccoon's low-slung body and short legs serve better than a human's for such ventures.

But the big advantage offered by raccoons was their value as trade goods. The continuing demand for fur in Europe kept the price steady on the frontier and provided settlers with an unexpectedly reliable source of income. A raccoon pelt, well prepared and of good quality, was as good as cash at any frontier trading post. Actually, almost no one had cash. Even government salaries and court fines were paid in coonskins. For instance, sixty pounds of raccoon pelts was the assessment against a man whose dog had killed a neighbor's cow. In the short-lived frontier state of Franklin—later part of Tennessee—the governor was paid in deerskins, but his secretary had to get by on 500 coonskins and the clerk of the House of Commons on only 200—and they were glad to get them. How much the skins bought in trade depended, of course, on how good the men were at dickering.

Prices were seldom fixed so firmly a little fast talking couldn't sweeten the deal for buyer or seller. However, Davy Crockett used to claim that in his day one coonskin was good for one jug of corn "likker" or hard cider anywhere in the west—which meant anywhere between Pittsburgh and St. Louis. And Crockett was also among those who liked to chuckle over how easy it was to watch for the right moment and steal back the pelt just traded and offer it again for a second jug.

Put Crockett's jesting aside and you have to conclude that the frontier would have taken far longer to settle down into towns and farmland if raccoons had not been so abundant. Yet hunting raccoons was never a sport, something done just for fun. Even when almost every log cabin had skins stretched out to dry on the walls, frontier folk usually had a special feeling of admiration for this animal that held so important a role in their chance for success or failure. How could they help but admire an animal who was so capable and often enough survived to old age in spite of all the traps and snares set for it? You could always tell an older raccoon by its fuller face, more rounded cheeks, and extra layers of fat. But the special mark was a graying face mask instead of black. The graying often started when the raccoon was five or six and increased with each year. Eleven or twelve years was about the full count unless the oldster was someone's pet given special food and protection.

Enough raccoons lived long enough to have a gray mask for frontier folk to make "coon's age" a phrase for any length of time beyond the normal. By the 1830s other similes and metaphors of raccoon comparison became common. You not only "cooned" your way across a log bridge on all fours. You also cooned for melons on some summer's eve, slipping out by moonlight to slurp over juicy pinkness fresh-picked from the vine—your own vine or someone else's—without recourse to forks and plates. Oldtimers, especially those who made their living as trappers, often referred to themselves in the third person as "this yer old coon"—a sort of modest way of boasting of their own survival skills. Somebody who didn't make it—but had tried—might be lamented with a shake of the head as "gone coon." Still, the number of pelts a man had to trade was the gauge of success. One protective frontier father with a pretty daughter was known to warn off unworthy suitors by declaring any fellow who didn't have enough coonskins of his own taking to make a decent bed cover needn't hang around making eyes at Susan.

In 1838 politics gave "coon" and "old coon" new meaning, for the presidential candidate to begin his try for the Whig nomination and election in 1840 was William Henry Harrison—definitely of "old coon" caliber. Virginia born, he'd pioneered in Ohio, joined the army, served as governor of Indiana Territory and won full status as Indian fighter by leading his men to victory at the battle of Tippecanoe. Then he went on to win more honors in the War of 1812 before returning to the frontier, becoming a senator from Ohio and a successful farmer besides. His rival for election was the Democrat incumbent, Martin Van Buren, who seemed to frontier folk something of a prissified dandy. So on the campaign trail the slogans pitted frontier soldier-farmer against city nabob, east against west, and a log cabin was the obvious Whig symbol for floats and banners.

"Just a log cabin?" somebody in charge of float-building had to ask. Somebody else, with a grin, plunked down a jug of hard cider beside the cabin door. Somebody else tacked a coonskin on the door above it. Nothing else needed.

One enterprising campaigner with a pet coon let it perch on the cabin roof to attract voters, but to all who knew the West, the coonskin was the right touch. And "Old Coon" was the right nickname to identify Harrison as the West personified. Everybody picked it up, boasted of having met "Old Coon" on the street, maybe passed by his house. One enthusiast who'd signed himself "whole Hog for Harrison!" promptly changed it to "Whole Coon!" Harrison won handily and Democrats began turning the nickname against him to ridicule the speeches made in "Coongress," and the "coonisms" spouted by new senators. Any Democratic victory was followed by boasts that they'd skinned the Old Coon but good.

There was little time for such diatribes. Harrison died a month after his inauguration, never to know that his grandson Benjamin would be elected president a half-century later and serve the full term Old Coon was denied. He would have been pleased about that. And pleased, too, if he could have known that in the 1920s two presidents would each have a live pet raccoon in the White House. Grace Coolidge, wife of Calvin, would claim the female she named Rebecca as special friend. Herbert and Lou Hoover, who followed the Coolidges in the White House, would have a female named Suzie.

Perhaps pet raccoons in the White House were a small protest against the killing of the mask wearers for coats for college students—the fashion craze of the Twenties. With 15 skins for each coat, raccoons were soon in some danger of extinction. Luckily, the fad ran out while there were still enough live raccoons in the hinterlands to rebuild normal populations. Some individuals moved in to trapped-out areas of their own accord while others were caught by wildlife officials and released where needed, the only time raccoons have required such replenishing.

Meanwhile, the great Mississippi River, so long a barrier against further westward expansion, became just one more river to cross for American pioneers. In 1803 President Thomas Jefferson, with masterly foresight and diplomacy, negotiated the Louisiana Purchase of lands once held by France and Spain. He then sent a Discovery Corps westward—headed by Captains Merriwether Lewis and William Clark—with orders to find a river flowing clear to the Pacific Coast. The captains were also to keep a journal of all plants and animals seen along the way, known or unknown, and of course the raccoon was among those most easily recognized. While the Corps was following the Missouri River through open plains, they saw few raccoons, but as soon as they reached woodlands raccoons were definitely abundant all the way to the coast.

Some forty years later when the great naturalist and painter, John James Audubon, was following the Lewis and Clark route up the Missouri, he was surprised to find Indians who did not know a raccoon when they saw one. Raccoons, so much a part of Indian life elsewhere, were scarce on treeless plains. He had a handsome old codger of a coon portrayed by son John in his three-volumes of North American quadrupeds published from 1845 to 1848, with descriptive text following in separate volumes in 1846-1854. His friend John Bachman aided with much of the text and his sons John and Victor did several of the portraits, but concept and planning were Audubon's own.

Proof that raccoons roamed coast to coast over the border in Canada had been established even before Lewis and Clark witnessed them in Oregon. The famous British explorer, Captain James Cook reported seeing then at Nootka Sound on what is now Vancouver Island, British Columbia, in 1778. A half-century later the explorer Henry Alexander would see them further inland, also, and mentioned them in his journals.

J.W. Audubon

The most detailed accounts came in the writings of Ernest Thompson Seton in the years from 1890 to 1910, especially his *Lives of the Game Animals* which was read almost worldwide. Europeans especially were fascinated by remnants of wild frontier life. One Russian reader would declare later that Seton's descriptions of raccoon fur, its depth, durability and warmth for caps and coats, led him to urge his government to import raccoons for naturalization. It took him five years to get action, but finally in 1936 twenty-two raccoons from zoos were released in a Russian forest of walnut trees and fared well enough, except in winter. Hundreds more were imported over the next decades, and this time artificial dens were constructed to give them winter protection—not always enough for survival.

Russians could at last wear home-grown coonskin caps, although they usually dyed the fur black and sheared it to look more like sable. Even earlier—1927—they learned caps could also be made from the fur of a very similar Asian species native to northern China, Korea and Japan. Now classified as *Nyctereutes procyonoides*, "raccoonlike night creature," and placed in Family Canidae among the foxes. It is known in Russia as "Japanese fox" or "Japanese raccoon" and in America as "raccoon dog." Although its fur is less durable than raccoon, it's a more valuable transplant because it survives Russian winters by hibernation—a trick raccoons do not need at home and apparently cannot learn. Russia imported several thousands of them through 1957 and many of them wandered on to Finland, Sweden, Poland, Germany and Czechoslovakia where they often shared the old furriers' *schupp* label with imported raccoons. Sweden and Poland now outlaw raccoon dogs because of conflict with native species, but both raccoon dogs and real raccoons survive in the wild in Germany.

Actually, some Germans once believed that raccoons had been native there all along. Many an old record told of a raccoon running wild near Hamburg in 1857 and after one was shot there right on Luneburger Heath between Bremen and Hamburg the report could not be denied. How even one raccoon managed to cross the Atlantic Ocean on its own remained a mystery for nearly a century. But finally Carl Hagenbeck, son of the founder of the famous Hagenbeck circus, confessed in his autobiography that by a most regrettable accident his father had been responsible. He had imported this one raccoon for a special exhibit and it escaped as it was being taken from the dock at Bremen to the family zoo at Hamburg. The

Hagenbecks had not reported the escape at the time for fear of public outrage at introducing alien species to German wilds, and had never had the courage to admit it later. But now that the father was dead and beyond reprisal, the truth could be told, a mystery solved.

In North America during the last century raccoons have been faced more and more with the problem of survival. A problem increasingly acute as the twentieth century slipped into its midway years. How could they survive if humans continued to take over more and more terrain? The wild woodlands that had always given food, shelter and territory to raccoons were vanishing. Whole tracts were disappearing, replaced by streets and houses, shopping malls, a maze of super highways with speeding cars, a never-ending menace. Where now could a raccoon mother find a safe place to raise her kits?

As raccoons have always done, they found an answer, a way to make do. Surprisingly, they solved the problem in two ways, with a retreat to more remote wilds or by adapting to city suburbs. Any suburban backyard with plenty of trees and greenery for refuge looked good to them—and all the better if there were adjoining vacant lots, a wooded hillside or culvert and perhaps a brook or frog pond not too far away. They made careful survey before moving in, making sure the people were friendly, perhaps judging by whether they provided food and water for birds, squirrels, chipmunks. And of course there could be no big dogs running loose. Any city with a leash-law for dog control gets the raccoon vote of confidence. Cats and raccoons, however, usually manage to get along.

So any family with a backyard to meet raccoon needs, then, may be lucky enough to have furry, black masked neighbors. At least that's the way it was for the author and her family nearly thirty years ago.

SEVEN

WHEN BACKYARD RACCOONS CAME TO STAY

ON A NOVEMBER NIGHT in 1960 my husband Lloyd and I noticed that Princess, our old white cat, was huddled with pink nose pressed again the patio glass door in obvious fascination. We flicked on the patio floodlights to see what held her in thrall and there he was—our first raccoon visitor.

Just beyond our narrow strip of backyard lawn a two-tiered red-rock retaining wall holds back the hill with its thorny tangle of blackberries and broom, leaving a ledge three-feet wide for flowers, shrubbery and water bowls for the birds. As usual, I'd added a few broken pieces of bread for the birds' breakfast and now discovered they made a raccoon's evening snack instead. There he sat on ample haunches, nonchalantly helping himself to another piece of bread with searching paws while he turned to look at us, black eyes flashing gold with reflected light. He watched us warily, yet never missed a beat in the steady rhythm of his chewing and we could not help but conclude he had been here before—more than once—and had judged us neighbors of good will. He had also learned that the see-through glass door did not provide a walk-through threat, for as long as the door remained closed he made no move to retreat.

When my husband opened the door to toss out more bread, our black-masked visitor headed for the bushes, not yet ready to give us full trust. But we were sure it would come—and it did. In a few nights we learned that his mate was ready to be a neighbor, also, and we dubbed them "Old Man" and "Old Mama," hoping that the coming spring would add kits for us to watch. Meanwhile, I headed for the library for books on raccoon lifestyle and history and made a notebook for our raccoon-watchers' diary.

Old Mama appeared with four roly-poly kits in June, and we had learned from checking those library books that they were probably about eight weeks old before she would let them get very far from her den door. Even now she didn't let them come down into the yard. The rock wall ledge was the limit of their freedom, but she did not send them into hiding when we came out with more food, and so there was some measure of trust even though they appeared only late at night.

I heard her often talking to the kits—a sharp "P-r-r-r-rt!" when they ventured too far from her side, a soft "Wh-wh-wh" of reassurance or comfort as they scampered to obey. But she did not speak directly to me until one night when I heard her growling angrily as I came out with another tray of bread.

"You growl at me—" I started to ask, and then realized that a gaunt black tom cat slinking toward her was the enemy she threatened. A stray, I thought, and perhaps hungry enough to try to snatch a kit, and promptly tossed the tin tray at his head with a loud "SCAT!"

The tom turned and fled and Mama rolled out an approving "P-rrrrrr!" in my direction. The kits had watched wide-eyed through it all and from that moment—I felt as time went on—they knew I was a friend, although they still came only late at night all through that summer, fall and winter. The following mid-April one of the kits appeared in mid-afternoon, the first daytime appearance for any of them. Rocky, we named her, because she was first of the babies from the rock-wall ledge to come alone. She was hungry, thirsty, extremely tired—and we decided she had just had her first kits. She ate, drank, sprawled awhile on the ledge to rest and then wearily climbed the upper wall to the lot above, which we had bought to give us added sanctuary for wildlife. Birds, squirrels and chipmunks were the wild neighbors we had counted on, never even suspecting that a creature so much a part of the wild as a raccoon would feel at home. We couldn't have been happier, though, and could hardly wait for Rocky to return with her kits after their eight-week babyhood in the den.

They came in the bright sunlight of a Sunday afternoon—Father's Day afternoon, much to Lloyd's delight—four, roly-poly bundles of fur, tumbling and stumbling over their own feet in their eagerness to keep close to Rocky's side. So eager they scarcely even hesitated as she led them headfirst down the rock wall, and only their whickering cries betrayed excitement at the challenge of the descent. Keeping close to Rocky was all that mattered and they came tumbling after her across the lawn to the patio door where we stood watching. Rocky looked up at us and her look of loving pride left no doubt that she had brought them on purpose to show us. And our own faces, our murmurs of delight as we clicked the cameras, told her we were as pleased as she was. Body language, as usual, said it all.

From then on all our raccoon families have come by day as well as at dusk and dark—any hour in the twenty-four during the years in which we had no human neighbors nearby. So it seems clear that their reported status as "strictly nocturnal," cited in encyclopedias and other reference material, is frequently altered by choice. Raccoons, obviously, see well by both daylight and dark, but their eyes are structured to reflect and re-absorb light for keener night vision, and when sudden light strikes out of the dark their eyes shine with an eerie glow.

Baby raccoons, with their pointed faces, fuzzy upright tails and furry bodies, look so undeniably cuddly and cute that anyone who cherishes cats, dogs or teddy bears can scarcely keep hands off. You will need all your will power to resist picking them up. At least we did. We have never picked up a kit or patted or stroked either kit or adult. We promised ourselves that we would do all we could to let them remain wild, as free to leave our yard as they were to enter, allowing ourselves only the privilege to share food and water—eking out nature's bounty humans have depleted—and to give them our protection from humans and other animals if needed.

In the first few years we did let them take food from our hands whenever they made the first move to do so. But we stopped giving ourselves that pleasure when we found they had begun to trust all humans—and some people were not worthy of trust. They offered food only as bait in a trap, sometimes hoping for a live pet but more often wanting a coonskin cap—especially in the years when TV programs of Daniel Boone and Davy Crockett made the caps a hero's emblem.

There was much trapping, too, in certain years when local newspapers headlined the danger of rabies from raccoon bites. Like most animals, raccoons can get rabies, but they are by no means overly prone to contract this disease. The Oregon State Board of Health reported in the 1970s that in a period of the past several years they had disposed of 90 rabid bats, nine foxes, four dogs, four skunks, two cats—but no raccoons. In 1989 state records still showed no cases of raccoon rabies since such accounting began in 1960.

Raccoons, however, do bite if they are mishandled. Biting is a wild animal's first defense. Even a gentle pet may bite the human hand that tries to reach for some food taken without permission—and bite again in retaliation for a punishing slap. Such bites are normal, natural behavior and by no means evidence that the raccoon is rabid. When our grandchildren wanted to feed raccoons, we made sure to teach them that raccoons are wild animals, not pets accustomed to discipline, and can be fed only with care and respect. But our raccoons took food with their paws, not their teeth, and we shared the thrill of winning a wild animal's trust without accident.

After Lloyd retired he took on the chore of refilling the water bowls each morning. They were almost always empty or clogged with mud from dirty paws. Sometimes they were upside down or halfway across the yard—evidence they had been used in some raccoon game. Even adult raccoons like to play, and the kits have endless romps that do much to strengthen muscles and burn energy. I have watched them wrestling with each other, chasing each other, stopping to swat an empty plastic container just to see it bounce, even rolling over on their backs to keep it bouncing in midair as deftly as a circus juggler.

The younger kits' favorite game is to climb up on mother's back and slide down again with a leap to pounce on her bushy tail. As they grow older, mother lets them know tail-pulling is no longer allowed. Every now and then some of the more enterprising kits would discover that the long garden hose trailing behind Lloyd as he re-filled the water bowls made a marvelous "tail" for pouncing. He'd feel a tug and look around, thinking the hose had caught on some snag, and there was the kit, head cocked, paw lifted for the next move, black eyes shining in anticipation.

Never once have they fouled our yard or patio with droppings. Raccoons, much like cats, withdraw to a toilet place apart from their regular sleeping and feeding areas, or any other terrain they frequent. In part, this need for privacy is instinctive, and the mothers reinforce it with careful training. From their very first visit to our yard, the kits were allowed to play or feed just so long, then the mother would give her signal for departure. In a short while they would usually return, ready to continue their adventure, and—as any former schoolteacher would—I quickly recognized these interludes as recess called for toilet training.

I was able to watch raccoons all through the summer, day and night, for my husband's work with the U.S. Forest Service kept him away most of the time. So Princess and I adjusted our schedule to the comings and goings into the patio and we left floodlights on all night so the raccoons would be used to them and we could see all that went on. The raccoons knew we were watching, but they usually paid no attention to us, seldom even looked our way unless to beg for more food. So our house had become the equal of any naturalist's observation blind, and I believe that what I saw in those first years was as close to normal wild raccoon behavior as any human is likely to know.

In April 1969 I checked my diary and found I had observed sixty-two babies from June 1961 through December 1968. By 1981 the count was 145 babies—though not all lived to adulthood—and there have been four or more babies most years since then, though they no longer come in the daytime. Some years—when dogs were allowed to roam—we saw neither kits nor adults. I did not at any time count any of the adults—except those first two, Old Man and Old Mama—for I had no way of knowing whether they were already counted as babies. We gave names to over thirty mothers that we could recognize, usually by some scar, torn ears or other distinctive marking, and sometimes by an individual quirk of behavior.

Professional zoologists like to make fun of amateurs who name wild animals, insisting that numbers—such as they use for laboratory animals under observation—are more scientific. But laboratory animals usually stay in cages and a number is identification enough. When you are watching wild raccoons by the dozen, each free to come and go, you need a name indicative of actions or appearance. So Raggles was the name for a mother raccoon with ragged ears—perhaps caught in blackberry brambles or torn in a fight. Hungry Hannah had an insatiable appetite, perhaps the result of loss of weight during a difficult pregnancy. Rikki-tikki-tavi had a continuing war with snakes—gartersnakes, of course, not the cobras of her name-source in Kipling's tale. The male that took over the territory after the Old Man vanished was Blacky—because he was darker than most adults, a common distinction among raccoons of both sexes.

With the mothers identified, I could see that they observed a careful protocol of patio rights. Rocky always came down the upper tier of the red-rock wall to the ledge, just as she had first come as a kit. She kept her babies with her on the ledge when other mothers with kits were nearby until she felt they had learned proper patio behavior. Meanwhile, Raggles brought her kits in by a path from the north and kept them to their own side of the yard when there was a third family from the south. At first each mother with her kits came only when other families were not in the yard. How they arranged this courtesy, I don't know, but it appeared that Rocky had first choice. When she left for recess, another mother might take her turn. Several times I saw a mother leave her own kits briefly and move over to take an identifying sniff of the other family, and by the next night these new kits were allowed to share the yard. If they got along, there were no further restrictions, although single-family appearance continued to be the rule at least once in a while.

Opossums and stray cats who turned up from time to time were tolerated and allowed to share the water bowls. I tried to comply with raccoon ideas of territorial rights by re-spacing water bowls at wider intervals—and feeding bowls, too—so that whoever came late could usually claim a private place. And before long, cats, opossums and raccoons were feeding in harmony on any night that chance brought them together.

Raccoon watchers elsewhere have reported skunks joining raccoons and opossums. One family from southern California found raccoons their first wild visitors, appearing every evening to raid garbage cans, dig for worms in the bulb garden and muddy ponds. When they realized hunger, not mischief, sparked raccoon behavior, they put out bowls of kibbles and soon had four families of mothers with kits in regular attendance. One night a skunk appeared out of the darkness. Tail arched high, it sidled up to the food bowl where raccoons were already munching. At just the right distance for aiming its infamous spray it stopped short and began a little stomp-step dance of warning. The raccoons got the message. Somewhere they had learned about skunk spray power and knew what a lifted tail threatened. Calmly they gave ground, merely daring an inquisitive sniff or two as the skunk—too short-legged to feed from the ground—plopped into the bowl, claiming tenure with full-body four-foot stance, head bobbing at a rat-tat pace.

With the skunk priority rights accepted, the raccoons now edged forward, reaching in for a kibble with careful but determined paws. Soon the skunks, like the raccoons, learned the bowl would be re-filled and they fed together in harmony. A raccoon might snarl at another raccoon poaching on its corner of the bowl, but not at a skunk. The smaller animal had a right that these raccoons were too smart to defy.

By day raccoons might also share the yard with Beechey ground squirrels or chipmunks that denned in the rock walls. Chipmunks were usually quick to cede territorial rights to the raccoons and scamper off. The Beecheys—about the size and coloring of gray tree squirrels but with an identifying black teardrop splash from nape to shoulders—thought they were fast enough to escape raccoon clutches. Evidently the raccoons thought so, too, for they seldom threatened attack as long as the Beechey kept its safety distance.

Of all this assemblage only the raccoons craved the sugar-water syrup we put out for hummingbirds and figured out how to get it. Just a twist and a turn of their agile fingers and the plastic-coated wire that held the syrup bottle to the firethorn branch was undone, the bottle tilted to their lips until the last drop gurgled down a happy throat. Now and then a younger kit would use different tactics, grasping the branch with all four paws and slinging underneath the bottle to suck away as he had at mother's breast.

But the untwist and tip-tilt method was the favorite and the young male we called JD (for Juvenile Delinquent) was the most avid poacher. My husband happened to catch him one day just as he reached for the wire.

"JD!" Lloyd called out with grandfatherly sternness. "That is a NO-NO!" JD paused long enough to assess the lack of real threat and went on with his tippling, tossing the empty feeder so hastily it splintered on the rocks. To spare JD cut lips—and restore syrup to the hummers—we moved the feeders to new hooks under the eaves where only hovering hummers could reach. No access for either syrup-sipping raccoons or bird-hunting cats.

The cats that come to our yard may be roaming pets or homeless strays abandoned on the hill. Both often end up in the county animal shelter and are given a mercy death if not claimed. Raccoons may accept them because they have no heritage of enmity for cats as they do for dogs, who kill raccoons by instinct and training. Also, raccoon kits are always looking for a playmate their own size, and most house cats happily oblige, especially if there's no actual contact.

The usual game they share is touch-glass tag. The cat is on the inside with the raccoon outside. The "pawtograph" proof of raccoon scoring is tallied by muddy prints on the outer side of a patio glass door. They also exchange sniffs of recognition and greeting through the patio screen in warm weather. Some of the friendlier raccoons would give this olfactory hi-sign to Princess when she was sunbathing in her patio chair on leash. They have shared games also with the three cats who lived with us after the fifteen good years granted Princess were ended, and other raccoon-watchers have also observed this cat-and-coon camaraderie.

Opossums seem to get only passive acceptance. However, when an opossum boldly climbs into the middle of the food bowl—because its short neck and legs do not permit easy reach over the rim—there's a touch of kindness in the way raccoons reach around its furry barricade to complete their meal. Once a big not-so-kind male raccoon nipped the opossum's flank and it scrambled out with a frightened squeal to take retreat behind the water bowl, but the kits who had been feeding with it kept a Peaceable Kingdom aura by tagging along to give the opossum a friendly "Are you OK?" sniff.

Opossums, as almost everyone agrees, are less than cuddly to look upon. But they will always be welcome in our patio because of one female I watched on a summer's night. She was drinking from the water bowl on the patio right outside the door, slinky ratlike tail stretched out behind her on the cement, when a raccoon and her kits came in from the north side. One kit came bounding up to the patio ahead of the others, spied that twitching tail and pounced on it with gleeful leap. Instantly the opossum spun around, long toothy jaws open to deliver a killing blow. But even as I leaped for the door, she had recognized her supposed assailant as a harmless playful kit and with a head bob of understanding turned back to finish her drinking. The raccoon mother was promptly on hand, too, and signaled the kit to follow her and leave strange tails alone. But she could not have been there in time to save her kit if the opossum had chosen to attack. Mothers are wonderful. Even opossum mothers.

In August 1963 the newsboy—who often stopped to watch raccoons with me—came to tell me that a raccoon mother had just been killed by a bus. "Not Raggles," he

90

said. "Ears aren't torn." So, then, it had to be Rocky and I was waiting for her kits when they came down alone and hungry at their usual five-o'clock feeding time. I'd put out bread for them, but someone else had eaten it, and though there was more down on the grass, they wouldn't leave the ledge without Rocky's all-clear signal. They were old enough now so that she let them come down to the ledge without her, but they could not go down into the yard without her all-clear signal. They hid behind the bushes while I tossed out a few pieces on the ledge and went back into the house for more. Now Raggles and her four came into the yard by their path, and since I didn't want to frighten them, I tossed the bread onto the grass. Whatever safety signal she gave her own kits, Rocky's orphans heard and accepted as permission to join the feast and down the wall they tumbled. All eight were so busy eating they seemed to have no concern for anything else, but when Raggles gave the signal for her four to leave, one of the orphans joined the single-file parade into the shrubbery. Raggles was suddenly aware of his presence and turned to challenge him with a short, sharp snap of her teeth right under his nose.

He knew that meant *scat!* But he also knew he needed a mother and he pleaded for her acceptance in typical canine beggar's pose, chin between spread forepaws and flat to the ground, rump high, eyes rolling. For a moment she did not move or make audible response, and then with a gruff whuffle of consent, she turned again to lead exit parade. Happily he bounded after her, last in line—but one of them. Meanwhile, the other three orphans had retreated to the ledge and took their usual path up the wall and into the brambles. Were they the bold ones in choosing to live alone? Or were they too bound by Rocky's training to disobey her rule? And which made the better choice?

Later when I made a midnight check I saw the three were still together, down in the yard eating hungrily, but not alone. Surprisingly, their father was with them, alertly on guard, not really at ease with his new responsibilities. Father raccoons normally do not babysit. They guard the territory from enemies, may join in the fight if female or young are attacked—so I have read but not seen—and let that be the limit of parental duty. Now I knew that the limit could be set still farther, yet not to full assumption of the mother's role. When the kits had eaten, he escorted them up the wall, but did not lead them as Rocky would have done. Still, I felt sure that he would be keeping watch over them in their regular sleeping place through the night. But what about tomorrow—and all the other tomorrows? They were still three months short of the usual time to be completely on their own.

The next afternoon the three came down the wall to their usual place on the ledge—alone. I was still wondering what my responsibility entailed now, when Raggles appeared with her four-plus-one. Instantly the adoptee was rushing to the wall as if begging his siblings to join him and they needed no urging. Raggles obviously expected them—no challenge this time—and she settled down in their midst, all eight getting equal attention as they fed together, reminding me of an old portrait of Queen Victoria surrounded by her grandchildren. Both her own kits and the adopted orphans must have obeyed the survival lessons she taught them, for she would come with all eight from then on to year's end when kits usually go off on their own.

I had read that mother raccoons sometimes adopt orphans, but I had found no description of how it was done. Now I had witnessed one way and a few years later I would see another. Nicky—always recognized by an odd-shaped nick in one ear—had been bringing her kits to the patio for four years by then and I was sure that this fifth brood would be her last, for her once-black mask was already beginning to turn gray. Perhaps she knew it, too, for when some boys set traps on the hill and took all four kits, she was torn with grief. She called and called for them, up and down the hill, crying out in anguish, and I could only watch and suffer with her. One night I saw her try to cut off a straggling kit from a passing family parade, coaxing with soft, pleading cries. The mother scrambled to gather up her straggler, snarling raccoon curses over her shoulder as she hustled it along. Nicky turned and fled back across the yard, and as she passed me I could hear her pitiful sobs.

I did not see her for the next day or two, and when she reappeared she had a kit with her, the two of them happy to be together. Had she found an orphan or—by some miracle—had one of her own kits found his way back to the hill? I would never know, but I did hear from a woman who lived on the other side of the hill who had bought a raccoon kit from a neighbor boy only to have it escape. At any rate, Nicky had a son beside her and the two were inseparable until mid-winter. Nicky herself did not have any more kits, but she would live well into her eleventh year, by then not a black hair remaining in her mask. Her teeth must have lost their strength, too, for she had difficulty eating dry dogfood pellets we put out now as a more wholesome menu than bread. One day my husband offered her a sugar cookie and from then on she expected one each evening—and got it. One morning Lloyd found a half-eaten cookie near her exit path and we never saw her again.

Meanwhile, we continued to be troubled with boys who tried to trap raccoons on our hill. One teen-ager, son of good friends and neighbors, even telephoned to ask permission to set his traps by our patio, trying to strengthen his cause by adding how much the pet store would pay for each one. I think I thanked him for having the courtesy to phone and ask, but I made no further attempt at politeness, barely managing to hold my anger under control while I explained how deeply he had insulted me by suggesting I turn traitor to the animals I had asked to trust me as afriend. And somehow he understood—apologized—and we became friends. Other boys came one night when they thought I was out, burlap sacks and flashlights in hand, cheering each other on to the chase as the raccoons skittered ahead of them into the bushes. I made no effort to hold my anger from them, nor did Lloyd, who happened to be home that night instead of out in the forest—and they tore out of the yard and up the street before we could recognize them. Luckily, city pet stores were ordered to stop selling native wild animals, but we still saw raccoons who'd gnawed off their paws to get free of illegal traps.

As a rule we seldom saw the male who claimed our hillside as his territory and the females as mates. As books on raccoon lore always explain, they are loners. But every rule is entitled to a few exceptions and Blacky—who took over the hill in 1965—was one of them. Blacky liked company. He loved his mates and the kits. He was down in the patio with them all through the year—not all the time, but often. When he joined a group he would greet each one with the raccoon salute—a sniff, nose to nose, not quite touching. And the kits would come rushing to him, begging for a pretend tussle so they could show how strong they were—or at least that's how it looked. He would promptly oblige, letting them dodge a few of his jabs or give him a poke, and then topple them over with a gentle paw. In courting season he not only gave the females his usual sniff of greeting, but would throw an arm over their shoulders for an almost hug. The females shared his attentions as they shared the patio, confident there was enough for all.

One day when spring was still around that unseen corner, Blacky showed us still another facet of his special personality. Somewhere—probably down by the frog pond—he'd met a scrawny, thin-tail Bachelor Boy who was desperately hungry. Raccoons store excess fat in their tails for emergency rations, and his bone-thin tail was proof no such rations remained. Blacky must have told Boy to come along for an easier meal than frogging, and I just happened to be looking out the west windows as they came up the hill from the frog pond together. I hurried to meet them, bread in hand, for I knew the meaning of the thin tail, but hungry as Boy was, his caution was greater and he dived for the bushes.

Blacky took his own survey for danger and then with a reassuring glance for his new friend came on to take bread from my hand with a thank-you pat—as always. He stayed only long enough to take a nibble to prove his trust and then turned to the bushes with a look that said more plainly than words, *See, this is a friend. Come, eat.*

Boy took one step but was afraid to come any farther and so I tossed the bread his way and went back inside, hurrying to find a curtained window where I could watch unseen. Boy came out now, Blacky staying beside him while he gulped it all down, and after a stop at the water bowl they went on up the hill. Before long Boy was coming on his own and for a while that thin tail allowed us to tell him from the others with one glance.

We had four nursing mothers in that summer of 1966, as I could tell by the swollen nipples, and I wanted to make a record of their daily visits before they brought the babies. So from May 30 to June 6 I settled to watch with time sheet in hand from 6 a.m. to 10 p.m. Blacky and Boy were visiting, too, and Blacky was still easily recognized by his red nape—the "henna rinse" effect males wear during courtship. Each of the mothers—Hungry Hannah, Raggles, Nick-nick and Patch—had a name to match ID clue, so I wasn't likely to make a mistake. Hannah came four or five times each afternoon, Raggles usually three, while Nick-nick and Patch didn't usually come until evening, although Nick-nick usually came once in the morning. Blacky was an evening feeder, too, usually, and Boy didn't have a definite pattern but came seventeen times over the five days—oftener than any of the others except Hungry Hannah.

Usually each female had the patio to herself, but once Hannah infringed on Raggles and another day on Patch.

Both protested mildly and then let her feed unchallenged, but privacy was again the rule when the babies began coming with their mothers. Nick-nick was first to bring them—four on June 5 at 9 p.m. Raggles appeared with three on June 8 and on June 16th Hannah brought four—but just two at a time, her usual precaution. That same day Patch also brought her four kits, two at a time. Neither mistrusted us but were taking care lest four lively kits at once be too much to handle.

If I'd ever doubted Hannah's trust, I would never do so again. I'd stopped making full-day tally but spent as much time as possible in the patio lounge chair with a sack of bread handy, sure Hannah would come with two kits. We thought she was teaching them to stay hidden while she was with the others—a needed lesson. One day she came with just two as usual, gently took bread from my hand as she always did, letting the kits splash in the water bowls or eat, as they chose. Suddenly a dog barked up on the hill, and she reared up, listening. It must have been near where she'd stashed the other kits, for with only a split-second of hesitation she nudged the two kits under my chair, gave a quick grunt probably a command for both the kits and me to mind our manners, and took off at a run.

I had just been appointed her private babysitter! So there I sat, scarcely daring to move. The kits sat still too, under the chair. I don't know their feelings, but I have never felt more honored in my life. Presently Hannah returned with the other kits safe and pleased at early rescue, and the afternoon went on as usual for them. For me it will always be special.

I had much more to learn about raccoon ways, many happy hours of watching, but nothing will ever stir me more deeply than Hannah's trust.

EIGHT

THE RACCOONS' YEAR AND ITS FOUR SEASONS

WE ESTABLISH OUR CALENDAR YEAR by nature's own schedule, matching it to the time needed for the earth to revolve around the sun. This comes out to a year of fifty-two weeks, with a few hours and minutes left over. We set our four seasons by the ratio of daylight to dark in each twenty-four-hour day. Spring and autumn begin with a day of equal light and darkness. Summer begins with the day of longest light, and winter with the longest darkness.

Raccoons also follow nature's time schedule to mark four seasons in a yearly cycle. By chance, this cycle tallies about the same fifty-two weeks as our own calendar, based on the time needed for a female to mate and conceive, to give birth and to rear kits to maturity—an imperative basis, for survival of a species is nature's only standard for success.

The four seasons of the Raccoon Year may be labeled Mating, Gestation, Rearing, and Hiatus. The last is a rest period for the female before a new cycle begins, as well as the interlude when yearling males leave home—willingly or by maternal rejection—and old males may find and claim new territory if they need to do so. Only the

Gestation season has a fixed time span. The others are variable. Both Mating and Hiatus may be shortened or lengthened by abnormal weather conditions, while Rearing may depend on variation in individual needs as well as weather. However, as a rule, the weeks are divided this way:

Mating - 6 weeks
Gestation - 9 weeks
Rearing - 35 weeks
Hiatus - 2 weeks

In the temperate zone, which includes most of North America, the scarcity of food during cold snowy winters gives best chance for infant survival if the kits are born in spring and grow to adulthood through the summer when food is plentiful. An adult female may come into estrus any time during the year, and so conception is possible all year long. But kits born in late autumn or winter seldom survive.

In the tropics the Raccoon Year will have much the same length, but it may begin any time. In the temperate zone most kits in the same climate area will have much the same birthday, year after year. However, variations will occur, and if a raccoon female doesn't conceive after the usual mating season, or if her kits do not survive, she will hunt for a mate and try again. Raccoon watchers may see those cuddly eight-week-old kits anytime. We've seen a few in Portland in September and October. Other Oregonians reported one in December, but kits are most likely to arrive them in mid-June where winters are usually mild, while those in colder areas (Maine, for instance, or Montana) may appear most often in mid-July. Rearing continues through summer and autumn and Hiatus, will come in December, as a rule. However, eager males often try for a head start, or if the resident male is killed or trapped for fur, females will have to wait until a new male appears.

Whenever the seasons begin, they will normally follow

the same pattern year after year. Watchers, therefore, usually know what to expect as the Raccoon Year unfolds.

COURTSHIP AND MATING

The female's body-functions mark the season's length, and so she is in charge. The male may make the first advances, but learns by experience that the female may or may not respond. Both male and female seem to enjoy a period of courtship, getting acquainted—or re-acquainted—and so they may do a bit of roaming together before actual mating occurs.

The female now has her den to herself. All the kits have left home, the males for a year or two of adventure and a search for future territory, and the females to await courtship and mating. The male now approaches the den of a receptive female and may or may not get his head in the door before a warning growl drives him away. If he is welcomed he will move in and the two will continue the courtship until the female signals that she is ready for copulation. They do not rely on a single mating, but will repeat their union several times. If there is a sudden heavy snowstorm, making forage for food impossible, they will settle down and snooze away the time together like a happily adjusted couple of any species. Eventually, however, the male will leave—perhaps at the female's suggestion—and find another mate within his territory.

If a female doesn't become pregnant after all, she will find her mate and invite him back—or perhaps try a younger, more active male. She must rely on the male to keep the territory reasonably free of enemies and so his strength and cunning are important factors in her choice. Usually only an older male—two to four years of age—is in the prime condition most likely to ensure full protection. So unless a female is desperate she will probably not choose a mate less than two or three years old. Consequently, bachelors may have a year or two to learn all the survival tricks they will need to defend a territory and acquire their own mate. Nevertheless, males are physically able to mate by their first birthday or even a month or so before. Females are ready at ten months and seldom have to wait longer.

During the courtship weeks the male may be especially eager to show his females how well he can defend his claim against their enemies. Big dogs allowed to run loose are now likely to have a run-in with a suburban raccoon. Even dogs in fenced yards may be attacked by some especially belligerent raccoon who does not understand that the barrier he climbs so easily will keep the dog at home. Other enemies to challenge his skills include great horned owls and other winged predators of similar strength and size. Also, foxes, bobcats, cougars, skunks, weasels and other mammal predators may be around, including smaller dogs, stray cats and certain humans who think coon hunting is a sport. Even hunters who only tree a raccoon and then call off their dogs can force a mother raccoon to flee so far from home her kits may be killed by other predators or fall into traps while she is not there to give them guidance. Danger and death for raccoons come in many forms, and the female has good reason to be careful in her choice of a mate. Once mated, however, she will not allow another male near her.

GESTATION

After the male leaves his pregnant mate for the season, she may re-arrange her old den to make room for her expected young or find a new one. Her first choice is a roomy hollow in a sturdy tree not far from water and food. A rocky ledge or crevice is acceptable, an abandoned underground burrow, man-made keg, box, doghouse or drain pipe with entry large enough to squeeze through (an incredibly small hole will do) yet narrow enough to defend with her own tooth-and-claw weapons, or any abandoned house or summer cabin with entry to upstairs, downstairs, attic or crawl space. Often storm-felled trees and bushes pile up together in a good den site.

Sometimes an older female has one of her own kits denning near her, and she may invite the daughter to share her den on cold nights, or to hunt with her now and then for the sake of companionship. Most of the time, however, each female is on her own during the nine weeks of her gestation and she will deliver her kits alone, also, with natural instinct her guide.

BIRTH AND REARING

A raccoon mother may have from two to six kits in a litter, but the most frequent number is four. Once in a great while there will be a seventh kit, but the mother has only six nipples, and since all the babies usually feed at the same time, somebody gets left out. The runt, who is usually smaller than the rest, most likely won't get enough nourishment and may not survive to go out on the first adventure with its siblings.

But runts do make it, sometimes. Clyde and Lou McLean, longtime raccoon-watchers in Miami, found a tag-along seventh kit among the babies coming to their patio one year. It was sturdy enough, but too small to reach up over the rim of the water bowl and get a drink. Frustrated squeals caught the mother's attention, and she quickly reached over to give it a boost with a paw under each armpit—the same help human toddlers need at park fountains.

Later when she called recess, the other kits went racing for the woods at a pace the runt couldn't match, and Mama picked it up gently in her mouth and kept going.

Newborn raccoon kits are fully furred, and though the face-mask pattern is visible, it is not so plain as it will be later. Their eyes are sealed shut, and their activity consists mainly of reaching, feeling about and squealing the first three weeks or so, with finding a nipple the only goal. They weigh only two to three ounces at birth, but by the time they are ready for first exploring venture at eight to ten weeks they will usually weigh about three pounds. By ten weeks they have their baby teeth, too, with permanent teeth usually in place at six months or so.

During those eight to ten weeks in the den—or just out-side the doorway for quick retreat—the kits strengthen their muscles with rough-and-tumble play and then col-lapse in a heap for a restoring nap. Almost always there's at least one among the kits ready to explore long before the mother thinks it's wise. Finally she leads them out on parade, always a little jittery about mishaps.

Her goal on this first outing is to find food they can learn to get for themselves. If the den is near a shallow pond or brook, she may make this first venture a lesson on how to catch a minnow, tadpole, salamander or perhaps crayfish (always the most delicious morsel for a raccoon). If a fishing hole or frog pond is too far away, she may hunt for earthworms and grubs, and the turning over of stones and logs on this search is always fun for the kits. Maybe a cricket or grasshopper will offer a happy chase. Early ripening berries or cherries may be visited, too, but many favorites—grapes, watermelons, corn, persimmons—are far from ready for raiding. However, if a mother raccoon has found a friendly backyard with water bowls and food bowls always waiting, she will probably take them there first. Her goal is to make the kits self-sufficient as soon as possible now, and weaning is part of the procedure.

Most raccoon-watchers report that they have never seen a mother carry food to the den and so they conclude that only mother's milk has provided nourishment these first weeks. That may be. Yet I have seen babies on first visit to our yard reach up a paw and take half-chewed food from the mother's mouth—take it neatly and without fumbling as if it is an action done before—and so I think it is possi-ble mothers may sometimes offer half-chewed food in the den. Also, when I happened to leave a half-loaf of bread—still in its wrapper—on the doorsill while I hurried to fill the water bowl, Hungry Hannah spied it and promptly seized it by the wrapper ends and hurried off, head held high so it wouldn't drag on the ground. Perhaps she meant it only for her own feasting—but kits were waiting in her den and she could have made a spur-of-the-moment decision to take advantage of this chance to give them solid food without the risk of leading them to the yard safely.

A kit on its first visit to the yard has already learned—or knows by instinct—that if it hunches up its body into more compact bulk it will be able to offer more resistance to the sudden leap of an attacker. Every hair stands on end to make it look larger, more threatening—and perhaps enough to bluff the attacker into retreat. It looks so much like the black cat on the traditional Halloween witch's broomstick that I call this pose "Halloween Hunch." Kits aren't likely to challenge me with such bravado except on a first visit, and they do so many other things only on this first discovery venture, I was determined to have camera ready for picture proof.

By now, with several families to bid for first-time privacy, new kits were most likely to appear early in the morning—usually before six o'clock. So my camera had been loaded and ready on the table by the patio door for several days, and I was awake by five, listening for the trilling chorus of baby voices that would herald arrival. And now I heard it—the *wh-wh-wh-wh* tremolo with the rising inflection of wonder and query as if they are exclaiming "What's this? What's that? Why? Why? Why?"

I was up and out and grabbing the camera—no wasting time on donning robe or slippers—and while two of the kits were busily trying to eat bread, the other two were threatening me with Halloween Hunch ferocity. Or perhaps it was the camera they challenged.

I got the picture—and several others—and sent them off with a background story to the editor of a well-known outdoor magazine. Back they came, promptly, with the comment from a new editor that she liked the story and wanted to publish it but needed pictures with a little more light. Same poses—they were delightful. But she'd send a professional photographer when I had the raccoons ready to pose again! I politely told the editor I could not make a date for picture taking with wild raccoons—that I'd taken these in my nightgown at 5:30 a.m. and more babies wouldn't be around for another first-time sitting for another year. Or maybe never.

The babies trying to eat bread like their mother were giving proof of baby behavior, too. Copying adult behavior is one way kits learn. One day I happened to be watching when a mother sat back on her haunches to eat—both paws holding bread to mouth in typical muncher's pose—and when her kit tried to do likewise, tilting back to make his spine as straight as hers, he toppled over backward and had to scramble up to try again with sheepish glance. But he did try again. You just can't keep a good raccoon down.

Discovering that water is meant for splashing is another first-time-in-the-patio thrill. Usually one kit finds the bowl first, puts in an inquisitive paw, pats, sees the water fly and pats harder, then jumps in with all four feet at once. The next moment a second kit makes the same leap and a third. Once I had camera ready when the fourth kit was too late to join the fun, and by the time he gave his all-at-once leap, the others had streaked off to obey mother's call for recess and he was ALL ALONE! There he sat in the bowl, looking utterly bewildered, with neither mother nor sibling in sight. Then he heard the call again and he was off on the run—probably never to be tardy for recess again.

As kits grow older they no longer fit the water bowl by twos and threes or—eventually—even alone. And they can't seem to understand why they can't curl up in a splashed-out bowl for a cool nap on a hot day as they used to. They try from first one side and then the other, step in front ways, side ways and any other way before they give up. I'm not sure they ever realize that kits grow but bowls don't. At least not until they have kits of their own to watch.

Other days bring other lessons. One of them is the need to kill crayfish, frog, mouse or any other prey that might bite back while being eaten. When a neighbor boy brought Nicky a few crayfish for a treat, we saw her sweep one out of the water bowl, slam it on the ground, slam it again, then dunk it in the water until her sensitive paws told her it was lifeless and could be eaten safely. I also saw Rikki-tikki-tavi grasp a snake just behind its jaws so it could not turn and bite her, then dunk it again and again in the water, squeezing it all the while until she was sure it was drowned and breathless, then cram its elusively dangling length into her mouth.

These lessons taught the kits to do likewise. They taught me that raccoon "washing" might well have begun as the only foolproof way to make sure just-caught prey was safely edible. So a kit's "washing" of sticks and stones might be practice or play. For adults dunking may help keep the sensitivity of their paws at its sharpest or may be the sign of a habit too firmly installed to break, even if no softening is needed. Or perhaps the reason is simply that some raccoons like well-sloshed food. Many of them dunk only food hard to chew.

We watched kits learn to climb up and down our rock walls, too, and up and down our big Douglas fir—both needed skills. At first the mothers stood by, ready to lend a helpful boost or catch an inept tumbler. Only later could they relax by the water bowl and watch.

Somehow, going down headfirst seems scarier than trying to climb up. Rocky's kits had followed their mother without delay or doubt. Others would start down, suddenly realize how far away the next solid ground really was and try to twist back up. Sometimes they made it. More often they fell, got up, shook themselves, looked back up at the top as if proud of success. Climbing up took more muscle power, for the kit has to pull its whole body weight up from one paw-hold to the next on the wall, one claw-hold to the next on tree trunk, and either can be tough.

Raccoons stand on two legs easily, with tails spread out behind for tripod balance—the same pose often taken by kangaroos. Now and then some child seeing it for the first time will ask, "Are raccoons a kind of kangaroo?" Of course they're not, but the tripod pose warrants the question. In 1696 sea-rover William Dampier, seeing tree kangaroos for the first time, thought they were related to raccoons. But while raccoons stand easily on two legs, they can take only a step or two before returning to all four. However, the print made by the hind feet usually obliterates those made by the forepaws, and so anyone reading the prints may think raccoons are capable of walking and running on just their hind legs.

In almost every litter there is usually a timid one, usually a male, who has to be comforted and encouraged and who always stays close to his mother's side. The bond between them is evident, and if by chance he is the only one staying with her as the Rearing Season draws to a close, the separation that must come is hard for both of them.

Other kits ready for Bachelor Boy status may take off on their own with no persuasion, often in a group—all the Boys from the area banding together for adventure and perhaps tagging along after the boss resident male to learn his secrets of strategy. The boss, however, has courtship in mind and will not tolerate the young males until mating is over. The females know this and know they must send their sons away lest they be killed or injured in a fight they can't possibly win.

One mother and her only son had been especially close, and she was always calling him to share some special food. This night he had been dallying up on the hill while she came down to feed, and when he finally did start down the rock wall, she suddenly halted him mid-step with a firm growl. He stood there, bewildered, then offered a puzzled query. She growled again—in stronger tone—but never turned to look at him. Perhaps she didn't dare. Facing me, she was a figure of utter misery, but the kit would see only her sternly turned back, hear only the growling tone.

Each time he took a step forward, she growled to send him back, and finally he just stood there watching her as she pretended to be intent on her eating, picking up one piece of bread after another. She left in another moment or two, taking the opposite trail so she would not pass the dejected figure on the wall. After a little while he came down into the patio, looked at the bowls as if he did not see them and turned and went back the way he had come.

That winter I saw groups of bachelors, as I almost always do, stopping by for a snack when no one else was around and then dashing off again. I never knew whether the young male I'd watched that night of misery was one of them. Here's hoping he found food somewhere, for October and November are the months when raccoons must store up fat to see them through winter, and one may eat three pounds of dry dog food in a single night.

HIATUS

Hiatus is the shortest of the four seasons in the Raccoon Year and the most variable both in length and action. For the females it is the only time free of responsibility and they may truly need it for rest and recuperation. It may also come at the coldest, snowiest time of year when foraging for food is difficult in the wild. However, raccoons have come to our patio for the food they've learned to expect even in deep snow, the thermometer below freezing, for they do not hibernate.

The yearling males need this time for finding companions to share their bachelorhood roaming and testing the bonds of their new freedom from maternal discipline. For the first time in their young lives there is no one to give a sharp command when they go beyond bounds. Can they now set their own bounds? If they can't, their chances of survival may be slim.

For the adult males it is a time of impatience for the courting days ahead. And for them all it may be a time of hunger due to winter shortages. If you want to know how wild raccoons are faring during winter hardship, look at their tail. All too often in these days of steady urban encroachment you'll see the bony thinness that gives starvation warning and adds a troubling question: *What next for raccoons?*

NINE

BACKYARD RACCOONS: WHY? HOW? WHY NOT?

MOST OF US WHO INVITE RACCOONS to our yard cannot easily explain why we are so happy to have them around. We know it's more than a vague fondness for wildlife. Yet it's less than a compulsion to save a threatened species from extinction. North American raccoons are too abundant over too wide a range to be in serious danger of disappearing any time soon.

However, the threat of extinction is there for all feral animals in the continuing loss of the wildlands that provide their food, water, and shelter. Anyone who knows the fate of the Passenger Pigeon has to be reluctant to predict certain survival for any species. In 1813, remember, Audubon saw those birds as "countless multitudes" in flocks so vast they darkened the sun. Yet only a century later the last lone Passenger was dying in the Cincinnati zoo.

It seems reasonable to conclude that backyard welcome will give at least a few raccoons more security than they might otherwise have. And the way they look up at you with those bright black eyes, once they have accepted your

Photo: Sam Dabney

Photo: Sam Dabney

Photo: Sam Dabney

Photo: John Pitman

Photo: Sam Dabney

Photo: John Pitman

Photo: Noel Young

invitation, gives most of us a heart-stir that has no price tag. Winning a wild animal's trust—for many of us—is all the reward we need.

If raccoons haven't come to your yard as yet, you may have more than a little preparation to make them realize an invitation is open. First you need a yard with some semblance of the woods-and-meadow wildlands. It must provide the shelter from weather and enemies their instinct tells them they need. Also the surroundings need untouched areas for den sites and natural foraging. Raccoons may accept less security if they have to, but something close to perfection is what they always seek. If you want raccoon neighbors enough to give them an ideal setting, you might have to go house hunting for yourself first. For you that would hold all the turmoil of deliberate upheaval. For us it was a happy accident.

When we gave up our roving ways and decided to settle down to stay, we happened to be in the Pacific Northwest—Portland, Oregon. Portland began as a pioneer village scratched out along the west bank of the Willamette River with dense forests crowding all around, shouldering their way up rocky hills and down fern-clad dells. The town grew as it could, up, over and around and through hill, dell and forest in the first years, and greenery remains everywhere in odd patches and unexpected turns. So we were able to find a newly-built house on a wooded hillside just within city limits. The real estate agent didn't know he'd made a sale the moment I saw a gray squirrel scampering over the rock wall at backyard edge and a rufous-sided towhee scratching for bugs under a clump of broom, but my husband knew.

The house was on a double lot, and we planned from the very first to let the uphill half at the back grow as it would, a sanctuary for every wild bird and squirrel that came our way. Feeding birds in a city backyard had been part of my life from the first moment I could recognize bird from bread crumb and I'd fed squirrels from my hand as a child, too. Having other wildlings at the door had been my dream since high school days when an article in *National Geographic* told of a city family who'd moved to a Texas ranch and found all sorts of furry neighbors stopping by for nightly feasting. Now, after years of living in big city apartments required by my career or the mining-camp housing to fit my husband's, the dream suddenly didn't seem so impossible after all. Luckily, Lloyd was all for making it come true.

Neither of us, however, had ever pictured raccoons as part of the dream. But here they were, and though some of our friends warned us they'd be a nuisance—even outright pests—we couldn't believe we could ever feel that way. And we haven't. For the first fifteen years of the nearly thirty they have been daily visitors they did not tear up our lawn, dig up our shrubbery or do any of the other destructive things we were warned about.

I must admit that a raccoon mother did re-design the row of tulip bulbs I'd planted in a curving line that crossed the path she'd established for her kits. When the leaves poked up through the ground as evidence of coming barrier, she rooted them out and swept them aside. Those not in her path remained untouched. I'd left her room for a new path, but she wanted the old one—and she was in the right. In emergency—the sudden appearance of a dog or human stranger, perhaps—each family needs to know exactly which way to go, no one getting in another's way.

We had no neighbors on either side of us those first years, and no one on the hill above us. The raccoons had plenty of digging room elsewhere when mice, shrews, moles, grubs and other burrowers were their quarry. Our yard was not molested. Our vegetable garden contained nothing on raccoon menu—just tomatoes and green peppers planted in among the flowers. Once or twice I planted lettuce, much enjoyed by the squirrels. But no one touched the tomatoes and I assumed the mothers had told their kits they were better left alone. Then one summer a kit decided to try one for himself. Or perhaps he just happened to bounce past and sent a round green thing rolling off across the grass. Of course he chased it, pawed it back into roll-away action when it stopped, even picked it up in his teeth, leaving marks. Every other kit on the hill agreed that green tomato rolling was great fun, so that was the end of our tomato garden. They harvested some of our grapes, also, but usually there was enough of this favorite fruit for raccoons, birds and us. Luckily we always have plenty of water bowls around the yard so that birds don't need to puncture the grapes to quench their thirst. At any rate, any damage the raccoons or other animals did never seemed too high a price to pay for their company.

Now that the neighborhood is developed and their hunting grounds are limited, raccoons frequently dig in our yard. If we had small children needing a lawn for play, or if a smooth sweep of grass were high on our list of plea-sures, we could not welcome raccoons so happily. But there are just two of us and a cat who never goes outside without a leash and who happily plays pat-the-glass tag with raccoons on the other side of the patio door. He even wakens me in the night if raccoons and opossums are there with an empty feeding bowl. So food and water are still out as a free come and go invitation.

In the beginning our first raccoons helped themselves to the bread we'd put out for the birds and so we continued with bread and other bakery goods. In those days bakeries sold huge sacks of stale bread and buns and broken pack-ages of sweet rolls, cakes, and cookies at a bargain price and we served whatever the sacks held.

We soon learned that raccoons go for anything sweet first. They'd hunt all over the scattered bits, pick up piece after piece and throw it down again if it were only bread—gobble it happily if it were a sweet. When they were sure nothing sweet remained, they'd eat plain bread if they were still hungry. As long as they had a choice, they'd reject rye bread—especially the dark pumpernickel—and hunt for white or wheat. Obviously, raccoons have taste buds and know what they like.

Eventually the bakeries were barred from selling those broken packages to individuals—not sanitary, the ordinance explained. So we offered dry dog food and have stayed with it. Raccoons like it and it is more wholesome for them than bread and bakery sweets, although they were disappointed at first. As most of us agree, eliminating sweets from the diet is not easy. And raccoons—who have never heard of calories or cholesterol—will not give up treats by their own choice. Humans who feed raccoons have to do it for them.

In some neighborhoods we know persuading raccoons to come to your yard instead of another has started an all-out rivalry. If one yard offers only dog food and others spread out a feast of fried chicken, out-of-season grapes, cookies or candy, there's no question as to where the raccoons go first. Of course, nature's sweets—such as corn on the cob, watermelons, peaches, grapes and any other fruit ripening in the neighborhood—will lure them away from backyard fare, too. But fruits do not carry the harm likely to come from too many feasts of marshmallows, chocolate cookies and other sweets not on nature's menu.

Occasional sweets may not do much damage, but it's difficult to know who else is offering such food besides yourself. Also, raccoons can be quite insistent about continuing whatever treat was first offered. Our friend Marge had her first raccoon visitors one night when she had nothing to offer but peanut M & M's. For several nights her supply lasted and the raccoons munched with glee, but when she offered only the plain variety—no peanuts—they took one bite and gave her an accusing look, stern black eyes demanding the "real thing" not this substitute. For apology she offered fresh eggs—beaten nicely in a bowl—which were accepted with apparent good will. But that's not a diet easy to fit into the budget for most of us. So don't start anything you can't continue.

Make a memo, too, not to offer salt-water taffy or caramels or other stick-to-the-teeth sweets. Some people think it's a real show—watching how the raccoons have to struggle to get rid of the clinging stuff. But there's too much chance of real damage to the teeth. And in the wild, good teeth can make the difference between life and death.

All in all, it's evident that people who want to live happily with raccoons—and want raccoons to share that happiness—need a clear understanding that sharing is a give-and-get arrangement. Everything isn't always perfect for either party.

Raccoons can bring hours of pleasure, but they also leave you with a few chores you'd otherwise be spared. They may tear up your lawn and flower beds hunting worms, grubs and other edibles on their menu. They peer in through glass doors and windows, patting the glass to make sure it's still solid and leaving muddy prints you'll need to wipe off. When their hunger and the odors from your garbage can lure them, they may claw the lid to shreds and scatter the contents every which way, leaving a mess for you to clean up. You'll be paying for a new raccoon-proof can, too—if you can find one they really can't open—and keeping it in the garage until collection day just in case it isn't as sturdy as advertised.

You've probably accepted the cost of dogfood as part of the budget, but may not be prepared for the bill restoring damage they do to telephone wires, fences, patio furniture (yours or an angry next-door neighbor's) and anything else they pull apart with those handy paws. Your budget may have to stretch to account for fruits, nuts and other garden treats you'd meant for yourself and for any prize bulbs or specialty fish missing from the pond after their visits. All these actions humans tend to regard as thievery or malicious mischief are well with in raccoon rights by wildlife standards, remember. So if you can't accept the consequences—or prevent them—you may be happier not inviting raccoons to share your yard.

116

Luckily, some of the damage can be prevented or at least lessened. Happy raccoon watchers in California report they've kept their Handy Paws family—and birds, too—from dining on apricots and peaches by covering each tree with sturdy, well-anchored netting. Some of their friends who breed rare and costly fish in outdoor pools have learned that an electric wire around the rim of the pool delivers a shock that doesn't really hurt the raccoon but is painful enough to discourage further raiding. However, experience has proved that some children are more easily harmed than others by such devices, and if there's a chance at all that children will come to your yard uninvited you'll want to rule this out even if your city hasn't already made them illegal. There's danger, too, in another suggestion from fish breeders—making the pool at least three feet deep so raccoons can't get a foothold. If raccoon paws are busy paddling to keep afloat—the reasoning goes—they can't be catching fish at the same time. But small children can't get a foothold either! Also, there's no firm proof that some wily raccoons won't learn to keep afloat with hind-leg paddling only and catch the fish with their teeth. The choice, then, seems to be raccoons or fish—not both. Unless the fish are minnows, crayfish, tadpoles and others you specifically intend for raccoon feasting. You may have to choose between raccoons and winning prizes at the county fair with your fruit and flowers, too.

If you're still ready to share with raccoons, a few reminders may ease the way for both of you:

• *Raccoons need to learn to forage for themselves*, so don't try to provide their entire food supply. Nature has programmed them to look for food in more than once place, and they need to follow that instinct if at all possible.

• *Raccoons need to remain wild*, free to come and go, so do not try to turn them into domesticated pets. Very young kits, used to their mother's care, will accept your touch without protest, but adults may mistake your approach as enemy attack and respond with a sharp bite. Then you are in trouble. Doctors are required by law to report bites from wild animals and a test for rabies is mandatory if the animal can be caught. The test requires killing the animal and if it proves rabid—or can't be found for testing—the person bitten has to undergo painful treatment. Make it a house rule not to touch raccoons, not to offer food in your hand, even if your raccoons always take food with their paws, not their teeth. If you've been handling their food, your fingers can carry the scent so strongly the raccoon may confuse your hand and the food. Once they have food in paws or teeth, NEVER TRY TO TAKE IT AWAY FROM THEM! They'll bite in self defense—usually without sparing time for a second thought. Likewise, don't even try to pick them up.

• *Raccoons have instinctive need for a toilet place* apart from where they eat, sleep or play. Usually it's just a little area near one of their trails. Mothers reinforce instinct by taking the kits to frequent recess periods, so it is well established. Raccoons confined to a cage are so frustrated by their inability to find such a toilet place that they lose all effort at cleanliness and soil the cage and even their water bowl. Of all the good reasons for nor caging a raccoon, that's one most convincing!

• *Raccoons need a den site,* not just for birthing kits but year-round. If you have the acreage, you may provide a hollow tree, hillside dugout, well-stacked brushpile, doghouse, cement culvert section wedged into rocks or hill. If you have no such accommodations in the neighborhood, raccoons aren't likely to stay unless they can find a make-do den within range. If they keep coming, you can be sure they've found a den—perhaps in the crawl space under a vacant house or even in an attic if entry can be managed.

• *Raccoons need professional care* if they have been injured or are sick. Taking them to a veterinarian yourself may be impossible, so call the nearest wildlife care center for advice. If you don't know where one is located, call the

Audubon Society, county wildlife commission or zoo for address and phone number. Your Humane Society may help, too, and sometimes will handle raccoons and other animals killed or injured by cars.

• *Raccoons have a strong sense of territory* and if you have more than one family visiting, you'll save disputes by providing several food dishes and water bowls with reasonable space between. However, after they learn that bowls are always refilled and there is no danger of going hungry or thirsty, they all tend to feed happily together most of the time.

• *Backyard raccoons may need protection from large dogs,* especially those of guard dog breeds. If any are near you, talk to the owner about keeping them at home. If your municipality doesn't require all dogs to be fenced or on leash, try to get such a law passed. Small boys—and sometimes grown men—think the best thing to do with a raccoon is to kill it, skin it and turn it into a cap with dangling tail. Some kill just to get a tail they can tie on bike handlebars or car aerial. Perhaps you can discourage such acts if you talk with school groups about raccoons as delightful neighbors, about wild animal rights to life. But some who ask about your raccoons may be thinking of trapping them, so check your property for evidence.

Along the way you may have to defend your beliefs if you are challenged by people who sincerely believe you are harming raccoons by providing food. Wild animals, they insist, are meant to forage for themselves, survive or perish. They tell you that kits who can satisfy hunger without work or developing their hunting skills, will not be prepared for life in the wild. They remind you that if the free-loading goes on long enough, even the mothers may fail to know enough survival skills to teach their kits.

It is true that wildling instincts are sapped by prolonged domestication, generation after generation, as has happened with turkeys and other barnyard fowl. But it is doubtful that raccoons free to roam and forage would lose their natural skills and instincts easily. You might, however, consider what would happen to the raccoons if you are suddenly forced to move away or if new neighbors refuse to tolerate them and force authorities to trap and re-locate them.

The same question could be asked of everyone who puts out food and water for the birds. Some naturalists feel that birds also are harmed by having too easy a food supply, no need to learn how to forage for themselves. Those who hew the hardest line insist that no food should be provided even if failure to do so means starvation during winter freeze and summer drought.

Most of us cannot accept such lack of responsibility for the wild animals that share our world. The birds and raccoons—and all the others in fur and feathers, scales and skin—were here long before humans took control. We have usurped their terrain, deprived them of food and home sites to satisfy our needs, and we owe them something in return.

One step is to provide fresh water for drinking and bathing. Almost no one will object to water bowls, artificial ponds or re-routing natural streams to bring them closer for observation of whatever wildlings may come to bathe and drink. And water alone will be enough to bring some birds and raccoons and other native visitors to your yard.

A second possible step calls for following the lead of author-naturalist-rancher Dayton Hyde who turned the family cattle ranch in southern Oregon into a wildlife sanctuary that his children and grandchildren—and friends and strangers—pledge to support through coming years. If the family business were growing fruit instead of raising cattle, the two would not be compatible. Both family and ample acreage are needed, too, so this isn't a step that everyone can take. But it does point all of us in a direction that might not come into our plans without his lead.

We can also help established wildlife sanctuaries make

better provision for supporting raccoons in the way nature intended. Few if any such sanctuaries have ample funds to supply everything needed or enough staff to do all the pruning and planting and re-stocking of ponds and streams that should be done, and volunteers are always welcome. Each sanctuary has its own needs and rules, but most of them would gladly accept an offer to plant a persimmon tree or two—if they grow in your area—or wild grape vines and wild cherry trees. Or keep a stream or pond stocked with crayfish and fiddler crabs—if the right place is available—or any other fish on the raccoon menu, even the kind sport fishermen label "trash fish."

Sanctuaries also need more suitable dens. The raccoons' first choice is a hollow tree, but few of them are allowed to stand. Next choice is a rocky cave or hillside burrow. If natural ones are not possible, artificial ones can take their place. Zoos all around the world have been successful with fake-fiber trees and gunnite caves as substitutes that not only look like the real thing but give real protection. And these are certainly more attractive to humans than the oil drums and barrels that have also been accepted by raccoons when nothing else was available.

Public parks and picnic places are usually designed more for humans than wild animals. However, a good many raccoons have already moved into such areas, relying on picnickers for food to help eke out nature's store. Almost any roadside park from California to Florida, wherever warm weather keeps visitors coming all year round, already has a resident raccoon population.

If you're traveling near Naples, Florida, you're almost certain to see raccoons at the picnic tables at Wiggins Pass, just a few miles to the north. A band of six—perhaps mother and kits—staked out mooching claim to a certain duo of tables in the spring of '88 and many a tale of their raiding prowess has been passed along.

The tables happen to be screened from the beach by scrub palmetto, but close enough so that picnickers can't resist plunking their baskets down on a table to establish occupancy and then dashing off to jog on the sand or dip in the surf—a habit those raccoons knew well.

"Don't let anyone take our table!" a pair of trusting tourists called one night to Floridians Dick and Doris McCann, already settled at their own picnic. Off they ran, leaving lunch boxes behind, not hearing the warning.

The two Floridians looked at each other. Raccoons wouldn't take the table—but they'd take what they pleased from unguarded lunch boxes. And here they came, swarming out of their palmetto hideaway and up onto the table, pawing, sniffing, poking, prying. Reluctantly, Dick clapped his hands and shouted. The raccoons scooted—and Dick set out to warn the joggers they'd have to come back and defend their supper or lose it.

The moment he was out of sight the six moochers were racing back. No poking and sniffing this time. They knew what they wanted now. They tore open the big red-striped box of fried chicken and, cramming chunks into their mouths, they took off on the run for their palmettos. Each one half-hidden by trunk or drooping fronds, they could munch in safety, black paws deftly holding up their treat for eager nibble while black eyes kept wary watch. They made no attempt to hide with their stolen booty. Evidently past experience had taught them that most humans would take no revenge—just stand there watching their supper disappear, shaking their heads ruefully and laughing—or digging into their gear for a camera.

All raccoons aren't that bold. One may come only to the edge of a campfire circle and sit there waiting to be noticed. If those in the circle want to make friends, and if they know something of the raccoon's role in American history, they may feel a sudden eerie tingle along the spine, a sense of no longer being in the here and now but somewhere back in time and place where human and raccoon once met in meaningful encounter...perhaps with

Meriwether Lewis and William Clark beside an Oregon campfire in the winter of 1805-06 as they marveled over seeing this old friend from their Virginia boyhood all the way across the continent, one ocean shore to another...or with John Lawson in North Carolina in 1709 chuckling over how fast raccoons gobble down fiddler crabs and crayfish...or with Captain John Smith in Virginia in 1607 trying to match the sounds of the Algonkin name to English...or with Christopher Columbus and his little clown dogs...or with a Mound Builder artist, half-finished raccoon pipe in hand...or with some ancient Indian puzzling over a furry mask wearer that might be spirit presence.

Wherever trails to America's past will take you, raccoons will be there waiting. And if all goes well for us and for the raccoons, they'll be waiting on all the trails to the future, too.

Photo: Virginia C. Holmgren.

123

TEN

RACCOONS AND RELATIVES—A FAMILY SUMMARY.

WHEN TWENTIETH-CENTURY NATURALISTS finally came to international agreement on terms of classification, they kept the old way of dividing nature's "world" or "empire" into three "kingdoms"—one each for animals, plants, minerals. Members of the Animal Kingdom are subdivided into stairstep groups called Class, Order, Family and Genus, each defined by the closer and closer likeness of its member species. A species is an individual kind of animal exactly like no other. It does, however, share certain likenesses with all other species in the same class and is still more like those in the same order, family and genus.

On scientific lists each species is identified worldwide by the same two-word label in Latin or in another language but with Latinized spelling and endings. With this binomial, any species can be identified, regardless of how local names may vary. The binomial is made up of the name of the genus (capitalized) followed by the name of the species (all small letters) both usually in italics.

In recent years some scientists have chosen to mark still

closer likenesses by creating a further subdivision for individuals called a subspecies. These are indicated on scientific lists by a three-word label (trinomial). Some lists also add the surname of the original classifier (not in italics) and enclosed in parentheses if his original label has been officially changed. For example, the North American raccoon is *Procyon lotor* (Linnaeus) on binomial lists but *Procyon lotor lotor* (Linnaeus) as a trinomial. A northwest subspecies would be *Procyon lotor pacificus*. Such distinctions are seldom made in field guides and other books for non-professional use, but it's handy to know what they mean when you see them.

Scientists also use a proper Latin label for each class, order and family. Raccoons are in *Class Mammalia* along with all other animals whose young are fed on milk from the mother's mammary glands. It is in *Order Carnivora*, "meat-eaters," with all mammals that hunt other animals for a good part of their basic food. Each family name is formed from the name of the most important genus in the group plus the Latin code ending *-idae*, "similar." Since the North American raccoon is by far the best known species in its family, the family name is *Procyonidae*.

Today when few of us have any chance of discovering a new species and getting our names Latinized for the label, we tend to make fun of all the old rivalry over scientific namesakes. However, a professional naturalist of a century ago had little standing, little chance of promotion, without such credits. And sometimes they were so eager for recognition that they based a new species listing on some minor difference in size or coloring—such as a little less black on a raccoon ear.

Even scientific lists sometimes omit species with such minor differences now. One most deservedly dropped was a raccoon discovery claimed in 1830 by British naval officer Edward Belcher, then in command of the corvette *Sulphur* on exploration survey cruise of the California coast. Someone brought him a raccoon with a mere stub of a tail, and he was ecstatic. A new species!

Fellow naturalists back in London agreed and it went on the books as *Procyon psora*, "mangy raccoon," a label suggesting the pelt had undergone considerable deterioration on the long sea voyage home. Why no Londoner guessed the stub was talisman proof of a battle with some predator or with a settler's guard dog is a puzzle now. Almost everyone who knows raccoons has seen bitten and bloody raccoon tails after dogfight disaster. But that wasn't the way it was in London in 1830.

This chapter lists two species of raccoons in Genus Procyon and four other close family relatives, each in a different genus, plus two others not close at all in spite of certain basic likenesses. The differences between these last two and the first six are so marked that each group is set aside with subfamily rating.

The six of closest likeness are labeled Subfamily Procyoninae. By common name they are the North American raccoon, crab-eating raccoon, coati, cacomistle, kinkajou and olingo. Their scientific labels and outstanding characteristics follow.

SUBFAMILY PROCYONINAE

Traits Common to the Subfamily: small to medium size, erect ears, large eyes, long jaw, prominent nose and nostrils; five-toed feet with non-retractile or semi-retractile claws, bare or semi-bare foot soles and flatfoot tread. They are usually omnivorous eaters, agile climbers, prefer a habitat of woods and water. They are native only to the Americas but two were first classified in Sweden, two in France, one each in Germany and the United States.

Early records: Because their native areas were first put on written record by the Spaniards, all six were in the sixteenth-century writings of leading Spanish naturalists as cited in each individual entry. For identification they are: Gonzalo Fernández de Oviedo, official historian of the Indies, who came in 1514 and stayed nearly twenty years;

the Franciscan friar Bernardino de Sahagún, who came to Mexico in 1529 and stayed until his death fifty years later; and the scholarly court physician Francisco Hernández who spent five years in Mexico in the 1570s recording medical uses of local plants, animals and minerals as well as many details on species names and behavior patterns.

NORTH AMERICAN RACCOON, *Procyon lotor* (Linnaeus) [Sweden, 1758]

Early records: As described in previous chapters, Christopher Columbus was first to put the raccoon on written record in his journal for October 17-18, 1492. His name for it was *perro mastin*, "dog like a clown," or "masked dog." Other early names and citings are also in previous chapters. North American Indian names are listed in Chapter 11, a glossary.

Clues and colors: Raccoons that keep to a single island or other isolated habitat over several generations with no chance of mating outside their group often inherit a mutant color that becomes normal for the group. Usually this is only slightly lighter or darker than the general coloring.

General coloring is a blend figuratively described as "pepper and salt with a dash of cinnamon" for western and midwestern raccoons. Eastern individuals are browner—cloves instead of pepper as the basic tint. Those on tropic islands are usually paler, while those on sea coasts who feed largely on crustaceans have an all-over rufous tinge. These must be the raccoons oldtime minstrels had in mind as they strummed banjos and sang of "the old raccoon by the light of the moon combing its auburn hair." A touch of auburn also marks males in courting season, inland or on the coast, and the reddish glint to their nape fur may last well into summer.

Young of both sexes are darker than adults, evidently a camouflage factor to make them less visible to predators peering into the den while the mother is away foraging for food. Raccoons, like any other species, may be born with little or no color—partial or complete albinos. More frequently there are raccoon melanos—much darker than normal, with little whiteness to the hair tips.

Size: The largest raccoons tend to come from northern regions where extra bulk enhances ability to withstand cold winters. For the reverse reason, smaller individuals tend to live closer to the tropics. Smallest on record are from the Florida Keys, Bahamas and other nearby islands. These measurements involve both length and weight, and in general indicate males are slightly larger than females.

Length is measured nose to tail tip—usually in the laboratory with a dead specimen or with an obedient pet. Average adult length has been set at 30 to 36 inches including 10 or 12 inches for the tail. Height at shoulder for adults is 9 to 12 inches.

Weight varies considerably with the season, especially in the north where raccoons instinctively overeat each fall to provide extra layers of fat to help them endure winter cold and hunger. Any October or November day an individual may consume two or three pounds of dry dog food even though experience could have taught that food will be available all year. Instinct speaks louder than experience in this case—and perhaps in others.

Unfortunately, most published records of raccoon weight are not dated nor classified as from live individuals or dead ones, wild raccoons or pets. Normal weight for live wild raccoons is difficult to establish. Several texts have listed normal adult weight as 15 to 25 pounds. Well-fed males in our yard look considerably larger and must be at least 20 to 30 pounds. A pet male from Vermont weighed 49 pounds, another from Wisconsin 54 pounds, and a fatso from Colorado checked out at 62 pounds.

Lightest weights of adults include those from the Florida Keys who tally only 3 to 6 pounds.

Weight for normal kits from average-size adults has been given at 2 to 3 ounces at birth. At the age of 8 or 10 weeks they have multiplied that birth weight sixteen times and tally 2 or 3 pounds. This is the usual weight of kits on a first-time foraging trip with mother or a visit to a friendly backyard. The runt of a litter—if there is one—can be much smaller and the difference will be noticeable through the first 6 or 8 months at least—perhaps longer.

Range and habitat: The overall range for North American raccoons is from southern Canada to mid-Panama—coast-to-coast wherever there are woods and water. An individual raccoon may claim no more than one square mile as its feeding territory if it has found terrain where food is plentiful. However, some individuals seem to have more need to roam than others, even when food is reasonably abundant. Also, raccoons whose territory is encroached upon by humans with their bulldozers and cement-mixers have to look for safer areas, and may travel incredible distances on their fruitless search. A raccoon terrified by hunters with guns and traps has been known to cover 10 to 15 miles in a single night.

An environment with woods and water is their basic choice, providing both the food and den sites they prefer. Lack of trees at high altitudes also keeps their range to no more than 5,000 feet above sea level as a rule, but they are seen up to 8,500 feet if other needed environment is present.

Additional species: Bahaman raccoon, *Procyon maynardi*; Tres Marias raccoon, *Procyon insularis*; Cozumel Island raccoon, *Procyon pygmaeus*; Guadeloups raccoon, *Procyon minor*; Barbados raccoon, *Procyon gloveralleni*.

CRAB-EATING RACCOON, *Procyon cancrivoras*, (Cuvier) [France, 1798]

Early records: As described in earlier chapters, the name of "crab-eater" was given by the Tupi Indians of Brazil in pre-Columbian times and was also used by other tribes. The first Europeans to use it possibly were Germans in Venezuela in the 1530s who translated Tupi *aguarapopay* to *schupp,* "fish-catcher," "fish-scrubber" or "scaler." A more literal translation of Tupi "leaper upon crabs and crayfish" was soon in Spanish as *perro cangrejero* and in French *chien crabier*—both misplacing the raccoon in canine category.

Drawing of Agoura, or Crab-Eater: J.G. Wood, 1865.

Clues and colors: Black mask and general coloring are much the same as for northern relatives. The pelt is thinner, an adaptation to warmer climate, and the hair on the nape brushes forward, not back toward the tail as with most mammals. The tail is ringed in dark and light tones, but the markings are usually on the upper side. In the laboratory or at very close range, observers may note that its teeth are broader than those of *lotor*.

Size: Much the same size range as *lotor*, although the body looks thinner because of thinner fur. It also weighs less, but is generally a little longer—or at least looks longer because of less weight and bulk. The legs are generally a bit longer than those of *lotor*.

Range and habitat: Northern limit is usually in mid-Panama where it may be in the same area as *lotor*. On the continent it stays east of the Andes and ranges south to northern Argentina. Like *lotor* they require a habitat with woods and water but are probably more dependent on running streams and large ponds because of their reliance on crabs and crayfish for basic food.

130

COATI, *Nasua narica* (Linnaeus) [Sweden, 1766]
Early records: Some Indian tribes used the same name for coati and raccoon when identifying these two for foreigners. But each did have its own name, and Sahagún, who spent a lifetime learning the Aztec language, makes the distinction clear. The raccoon , he wrote, was *mapachitli,* "one who takes everything in hand"—and its near look-alike was pesotli, "greedy one," whose paws weren't as similar to human hands as *mapachitli.* The Aztec name is still used throughout much of Central America but Sahagún's remarkable book was not published until the nineteenth-century and so another Franciscan, André Thevet of Paris, was first with name and description on a printed page. His book on the "singularities" he saw in Brazil was published in Paris in 1558 and in English in London ten years later, giving the Tupi name *coati* double exposure. In Tupi, *coa* means "belt" or "strap"—any flexible length of tanned leather or woven fibres—and *ti* means "nose," "snout." So "one with flexible snout" is coati meaning—a perfect fit. That beltlike nose can twist to right or left, up or down, in something close to a 45 degree arc and it becomes a food-gathering tool every bit as agile as *mapachitli* paws.

Drawing: Lumden, 1794.

131

PROCHYON, Storr. Canine teeth large, and compressed on one side ; grinders $\frac{6-6}{6-6}$, the first three pointed, the three hinder tuberculated ; muzzle pointed ; ears small ; tail long, pointed ; stand on the heel of the hinder legs, but walk on the toes ; mammæ six, ventral. *Ursus Lotor*, L. Racoon (*fig.* 165.). 2 sp. N. America.

165   166

NASUA, Storr. Teeth of the last ; muzzle elongated ; nose moveable ; feet semipalmate ; nails strong ; tail long. *Nasua rufa* (*fig.* 166.). 2 sp. S. Am.

Drawing: Swainson, 1838

Watching that twistable nose in action is always a good excuse for laughter, and so in various Indian languages the name or nickname meant "clown" or "funny one." When the Dutch arrived in the Guianas, they dubbed it "clown," too—*quasjic*—a name you still hear. In Nicaragua, *chollo* has much the same meaning, and kits are often taken when still nursing to become family pets.

In spite of Europe's early acquaintance with the word, the animal itself was not often seen alive there. Linnaeus saw his first skin barely in time to enter it in the twelfth edition of his famous *Systema Naturae* in 1766. The prominent nostrils—bulging, black and shiny—struck him as the feature worth specific label and so he published it as *narica*. But instead of putting it in the genus of bears, as he did raccoons, he enrolled it as *Viverra narica*, with weasels, civets, ferrets. It does look like the African civet, which also has a dark mask and ringed tail, but has very different behavior patterns and no hint at all of the trademark flexible snout. Obviously Linnaeus did not know how flexible that snout could be. And he was probably unaware that he was not the first to give this Indies animal its civet label. Back in 1601 Samuel de Champlain, just returned from his first voyage to the New World, described a long-nosed, ring-tailed Indies animal and sketched its picture and labeled it *civette*. So the coati carried double listing in civet category until 1780 when the German classifier Gottlieb Storr revised Linnaean errors for both coati and raccoon. Storr placed each in its own genus, and his *Nasua narica*, "one of the nose and nostrils," still stands.

Meanwhile, another early record added further confusion. The German naturalist Georg Marcgrave, who wrote of Brazilian wildlife in 1698, insisted the full name was *coati-mundi*. Later research proves this means "solitary coati" and therefore indicates only the male. Males are indeed loners except in courting season, and so the distinction is accurate and useful when properly applied. Even today, many do not understand the difference between the two names from the ancient Tupi language. Furthermore, older books—such as Michelson's *Merchants Polyglot Mannual* of 1862—may still present coati as another name for raccoons.

Clues and colors: A coati does not have the low-set outer toes that give the raccoon its almost-human grasp. Facial markings are not so distinct, tail longer, but not so bushy. But even at a distance the longer snout is clue enough for most watchers. An additional clue is the silhouette with the tail almost always carried high in the air. Coatis are especially agile tree climbers and will leap for the high branches at first alarm, scampering from one to another as easily as if on solid ground. If cornered, they hiss and spit, flicking the tail from side to side in warning that attackers had better keep their distance. The warning should be heeded, for those who know coati strength insist they can almost always outfight a dog.

At close range you will see the coati lacks the "pepper-and-salt" coloring of the raccoon and is furred in varying shades of brown and beige, with the lighter tints sometimes almost orange.

Size: Overall length for adults ranges from 4 to 4-1/2 feet, the body longer and slightly thinner than a raccoon's. Females are slightly smaller than males and the tail accounts for more than half the total length. Newborn coatis are much like raccoon babies in size and growth pattern. There are usually 4 or 5 to a litter and they are kept in the den for 5 or 6 weeks before allowed to learn foraging behavior and outdoor safety rules.

Range and habitat: Coatis are at home from southwestern states on down through Mexico and Panama to South America in forest regions. They may co-exist with raccoons as far south as central Panama, and from Panama further south they are neighbors to the crab-eating raccoons. In Panama all three may be seen on a single day. All three may also be seen in some of the larger zoos of both Europe and the Americas, but European signposts may not identify them by their American names. The old Linnaean label of "wash bear" still persists for the raccoon in many countries and bear genus has been extended to the whole subfamily group. In German zoos the sign to follow points to *Kleinbärren*, "little bears," and the coati is *nasenbär*, "nose bear," or *russelbär*, "snout bear," although Latin binomials—if given—will be correct.

Additional species: Cozumel Island Coati, *Nasua nelsoni*; Mountain Coati, *Nasuella olivacea*.

CACOMISTLE, *Basariscus astutus* (Lichtenstein) [Berlin, 1827]

Early records: This small catlike denizen of rimrock hill country was first described for European readers by the Spanish naturalist Oviedo in 1535. He called attention to the handsome ringed tail—as everyone still does—and added that the species was native both north and south of Mexico, for it had been seen by Hernando De Soto and his companions on their arduous northern trek.

De Soto had described the sharply distinct white and

black bands of the tail as *sierras*—a word that unfortunately has several meanings. Instead of recognizing the comparison to sharp ridges, Oviedo—or some of his readers—thought the tail had sharp teeth like a saw. Since most Europeans of the sixteenth century fully believed anything could happen in America, they marveled at an animal that could slice through branches and tree trunks with a swish of its saw-edged tail. Just one of the many travelers' yarns that were started without any intention to deceive.

J.J. Audubon

In mid-century Sahágun recorded its two Aztec names: *itzcuinquani*, "night howler," and *cuitlamiztli* (also spelled *tlaco-miztli*) meaning "little hisser." The original full-size *miztli* is the mountain lion and so the name points to the feline likeness almost everyone is sure to notice. With a few centuries of use, the Aztec name acquired its present spelling although

135

the meaning has been lost even for most of those who manage to remember the unfamiliar syllables.

In the 1570s the Spanish physician-naturalist Francisco Hernández would hear a third name for the little hisser—*tepe-maxtlaton*, "little white-banded mountain dweller." The white bands are on both face and tail to make the name a helpful ID clue, and Hernández added that in general anatomy the banded one was something between a house cat and a weasel. He also praised the devotion of parents to their young, so he must have known that both parents bring the kits food, with the father taking responsibility as well as the mother—a sharing not usual with others in the family.

As more Europeans came to the Americas, the cacomistle acquired a ragbag collection of names in various languages. In U.S. southwest it was often dubbed "miner's cat." House cats weren't available until Europeans brought them and this "hisser" was the right size, had the right persistence in catching mice, rats and other small pests, to make the perfect substitute as miner's pet and vermin catcher. The ringed tail suggested raccoon relationship to some while others saw a likeness to a fox and still others thought the banded tail itself deserved namesake mention. So the names you'll read in old pioneer journals include "coon cat," "fox cat," "band-tailed cat," "ring-tailed cat," even "ring-tailed coon-cat"—as well as "civet cat." Many North American naturalists insist "ring-tail" is a better name than tongue-twisting cacomistle any day—and they use it in their books and articles regardless of official preference for the modernized version of the Aztec word.

Martin Lichtenstein, founder of the Berlin zoo, who was first to give this species its official listing, classified it in a genus named for its foxlike pointed face and general shape of its skull as well as the foxlike way it flaunted its bushy tail. He seconded the likeness to fox cleverness with specific name *astutus* in praise of its ability to survive in harsh surroundings.

"Ring-tail" was the name artist-naturalist Audubon

chose in 1848 when he and his son John added this foxy clever one to their book on North American quadrupeds. He told of its adaptability in nesting in rocky caves when favorite hollow oak trees were not at hand, and he noted how cannily they chose a den with good coverage from thorny undergrowth that animal or human raiders could not easily penetrate. Audubon also commented on their sharp teeth, used to gnaw den openings to the right width, and perhaps this gives us a clue that the old yarn about the sharp edged "saw-tooth" tail might have come from some unnoticed printer's error in Oviedo's book, some word added or omitted that would have made the meaning clear.

Clues and colors: The long bushy ringed tail has an equal number of black and white bands—7 or 8 of each. The sharp dividing lines are not so clear on the underside as on top—perhaps a camouflage trick when the tail is curled around a sleeping cacomistle inside a den. The body is fawn-colored—lighter-toned below than on the back—and slender, sleek, lithe in graceful movement. It has a some-what musky anal scent (as do most Procyonines to some degree) and it also has the prominent nostrils that are a sub-family trait. Black muzzle with white bands above and below also serve as a reminder of Procyonine category.

Kits are born in May or June—one to five in a litter. The markings on tail and face are faintly visible beneath their birthdown fuzz. Both parents bring meat to the den while the kits are still nursing, and almost as soon as their eyes are open (4-1/2 to 5 weeks) they are taught to go outside for their toilet needs so the den stays clean. At 8 or 10 weeks they begin to hiss at any intruder instead of issuing their previous babyish squeaks, clearly living up to their Aztec name.

Size: The usual description is "house cat size" for both kits and adults. Adult measurements give length as 24 to 34 inches with at least half of that provided by the tail. Weight will be less than that for well-fed house cats. There may be plenty of fat cats, but there's no such thing as a fat cacomistle. At least not in the wild.

Range and habitat: Habitat, as a rule, is rocky hill country but open woodlands of oak and pine are also tolerated. So are abandoned ruins of long-vanished pueblo tribes who had the same need for nearby water that cacomistles require. The general range is usually given as extending from southern California to eastern Texas in the United States, but individuals frequently range beyond those boundaries and have been seen now and then as far north as southern Oregon. Beyond the Rio Grande they are at home all down the isthmus and well into South America.

Additional species: Central American cacomistle, *Bassaricyon sumichrasti.*

KINKAJOU, *Potos flavus*, (St. Hilaire & G. Cuvier) [France, 1795]

KINKAJOU, OR POTTO.—*Cercoleptes caudivólvulus.*

J.G. Wood, 1865

Early records: The kinkajou looks and acts so much like the olingo (see next entry) that early records do not always make it clear which was described. Probably both were among the "little bears" seen by Amerigo Vespucci in 1500 as he explored Venezuelan shores. Both are still

138

seen there and watchers still smile at the teddy-bear like-ness of pert face and soft fur standing upright like a crew-cut on the crown.

In spite of similar size, shape and color, there is one way to tell the two apart—if you're close enough to touch the crew-cut mane. Kinkajou fur brushes two ways smoothly forward from shoulder to crown backward from shoulder to tail. Olingo fur smooths backward all the way. So when Oviedo wrote of seeing a little night-roving *bivana* with fur that grows both ways he established his claim as first among Europeans to put the kinkajou on written record in 1535. The name *bivana* is no longer used and its meaning is apparently lost, but the kinkajou has plenty of other names in every language within its tropic homeland.

A second way to tell kinkajou from olingo was cited by Hernández in the 1570s although neither he nor Oviedo realized they had two species. "Clever hands much like the *mapachitli*," Hernández noted, giving the kinkajou its Aztec name *cuauhtenzo*, "tree climber," "tree dweller." "A very tame animal," he added, "prankish...feeds on bananas and other fruit...it is of the woods-weasel kind and has a very long tail." Though he noticed the kinka-jou's manual dexterity (which olingos lack) and tail length, he missed another clue in the olingo-or-kinkajou riddle.

The olingo has a long tail but it differs from the kinka-jou's in one factor many Europeans continued to miss right on through the nineteenth century. The kinkajou's tail is prehensile. It can curl around any jutting twig or branch with a once-around hold or even a double-curlicue twist. Although the olingo tail may swish with a graceful curve, and is well-furred, it usually hangs down as straight as any rat tail and can never manage the kinkajou's wrap-around grip. So the kink in the kinkajou tail makes for instant distinction between these two look-alikes.

The role of naming the kinkajou goes to the great French naturalist Buffon. In 1766 a friend from Jamaica sent him a drawing while another correspondent sent a description, giving it Indian names that sounded like *cacajao* or *sapajou*. At the same time he had reports of a furry tree-climber from French-Canada called something like *carcajou* or *quincajou*. Completely forgetting how far apart these two areas are and how unlikely that tribes living at such a distance from each other would speak the same language, he decided that quincajou was the one name to become official for the tropic tree-climber and entered it in his world famous *Histoire Naturelle*.

To ease pronunciation problems for Europeans, Buffon changed the spelling to kinkajou and felt the issue settled—until he learned that *quincajou* is an Algonkin name for the wolverine—a much larger species with little resemblance to the kinkajou except that both are known for a voracious appetite. Buffon apologized for his mistake in his next edition, but by then his spelling was in international use, for Buffon's reputation guaranteed prompt acceptance. And so the name remains.

The kinkajou's scientific genus—*potos*—is due to another mistake. African slaves in the Caribbean took one look at the "little bear" and mistook it for a similar-looking African lemur they'd often kept as a pet. The lemur is not related and has a much shorter tail, but big kinkajou eyes and soft fur were a reminder of the African *potto*. Europeans who had never seen the African animal accepted it as a correct name—and *potto* it is still used for the kinkajou by many people to this day. *Flavus*—the species name—means yellow, not a perfect choice for the lush redgold hue of kinkajou coat.

Another wrong choice is "honey bear," since kinkajous are not bears. But—like all Procyonids—they do love honey and feast on it often since the wild bees of their homeland have no sting. As any watcher soon learns, they dip into the honey with agile paws and even more agile tongue which can either curl up at both sides to form a useful spoon, or flatten out to become a tidy wash cloth. Whatever kinkajou's eat, they go at it with such gusto that several Indian names—*cuchumbi*, for one—mean "little greedy."

Clues and colors: Clues and colors are so interwoven with the early records little needs to be added. Kinkajou fur color varies from one district to another—more reddish here, more golden somewhere else. Prehensile tail, forward-bending hair from nape to crown and agile hands distinguish it from the olingo. A pointed snout separates it from round-faced monkeys of similar size and equally curlicue tails.

Size: Except for the longer prehensile tail, general body shape and size are those of a house cat. Overall length is around 36 inches, at least half of which is the tail. Some tails of 24 inch length have been reported. Its legs are shorter than those of the olingo and its body somewhat plumper—evidence that its extra energy demands extra reserves.

Range and habitat: Kinkajous are at home in tropical rain forests from Mexico down across the isthmus to Venezuela and east to Matto Grosso, Brazil. They nest in tree-hole dens, feed almost entirely in the treetops and only occasionally come down to the ground for fallen fruit or some other tidbit. They rely on treetop escape routes for defense against the rain forest's many predators and as the forests are depleted, the kinkajous will become seriously threatened. They are largely night creatures, seldom seen by day, as Oviedo noted, and they are frequently taken as pets, lured into captivity by their enormous appetites, especially for sweets.

Unfortunately they also like liquor, and tropical drinks with both liquor and fruits are favorites. Pet kinkajous who have made themselves at home in some tropical bar often hide in the rafters ready to drop down and slurp up a drink before the unwary tourist has a chance for a sip—better than any floor show for bar regulars who know what's coming.

Kinkajous are shown in many zoos. In Germany their

label reads *wickel-bär,* "wrap-around bear." If sold as pets they often escape to roam in suburban areas and turn beggar at some convenient door when hunger insists. They also get into considerable mischief, can bite the hand that doesn't feed them quickly enough and are far happier in the forest than in a cage.

OLINGO, Bassaricyon gabbii (J.A. Allen) [U.S.A., 1876]

Olingo: Huet,1883.

Early records: Olingos were the last of this family to be put on scientific records because European classifiers did not believe they were a true species. Nineteenth century naturalists argued—sometimes vehemently—over whether kinkajous have a prehensile tail. A straight-tailed pet was exhibited as proof of one side of the disagreement by those who never realized two species were involved.

Nevertheless, the Spanish naturalist Oviedo had seen both species early in the sixteenth century and though he didn't realize he had two similar looking species, he did describe each by a feature the other does not share. For the kinkajou, it was the two-way fur. For the olingo it was the offensive stench of its anal spray. *"Un hedor incomparable!"* he called it, no doubt twitching his nostrils wryly at memory of this "unmatchable stink."

Oviedo identified this stinker as a *zorillo*, "little fox," a catchall term for almost any small animal with pointed face until some pronounceable Indian name could be adapted. The Franciscan friar Sahagún supplied the Aztec name *ocotochtli*, "agile one," which perhaps should have been *ocuahtochtli*, "agile one of the trees," for on Spanish tongues it softened into *cuataquil*—a name still used in Central America.

Sahagún evidently never had to dodge the agile one's anal spray, and he must have misunderstood the Aztec who told him about its disastrous effect on pursuing predators, for he described it as a "vile fluid" which came from the animal's tongue. He was right, however, in saying that the target was the pursuer's eyes. The spray can cause instant blindness and acute pain, and leave the blinded one writhing in anguish while the olingo runs for its treetop escape routes.

To the Aztecs, this fluid was magic, proof of the olingo's link with spirit powers. They said it was a slave to larger predators who would lurk nearby, ready to feast on whatever creature lay blinded and helpless. No doubt predators did just that, and the Aztecs would have been convinced that only a slave would provide food for others. Later two other Spanish naturalists—the friar Alonso de Molina and the physician Hernández—would repeat this tale of fact masquerading as magic. Perhaps they half-believed it, for they apparently made no search for the truth of the olingo's power. Hernández did follow through with his usual scientific thoroughness and noted that this new animal had hairy tufts on the soles of its feet—not a common trait. In his own book of rules he had already declared foot structure an important factor in establishing inter-species relationships, and he placed this little Indies prowler in Family Dasipodidae, "hairy-footed ones." He made no record of the anal spray of unmatchable stink, however.

The olingo spray power escaped documentation for so long because it fades rather quickly. Only someone right on the scene suffers its full force. Luckily for us, Dr. Ivo Poglayen, formerly director of the Louisville Zoological Gardens, has been on the scene, for he had as many as twenty olingos at a time in his home for observation. Apparently the olingo is so confident in its ability to outrun larger predators that it sprays only when it has no other chance of escape, Poglayen states. He adds that the resultant carrion-like stench is so nauseating that skunk spray seems perfume in comparison.

Official classification as a separate species finally came in 1876 when The Smithsonian Institution received a specimen taken in Costa Rica by William Gabb, an experienced collector who recognized its unique features. The Smithsonian published a description under the binomial *Bassaricyon gabbii*. The species name honors the collector, and the generic label is a Greek combined form for "fox-dog" and points to kinship with cacomistles (Genus Bassariscus) and raccoons (Genus Procyon).

Professor Gabb had not included a common name in either Spanish or any Indian language, and The Smithsonian allowed its new entry to wear only its scientific binomial for the next forty years. A French scientific magazine publishing its picture in 1882 simply labeled it *Bassaricyon* and other texts—even dictionaries—followed suit.

In 1920 Edward A. Goldman of the U.S. Biological Survey decided to end this ambiguity and arbitrarily chose one of the many folk names he had heard in Panama. Any one of a dozen or so was just as right as any other, but "olingo" was seldom used for the kinkajou and so seemed the least confusing choice. Publication in a Smithsonian *Bulletin* made it official and eventually it was used by both British and U.S. zoos.

Oddly, no British or U.S. dictionaries would include this word until nudged to action by the author's query. But after asking for further research, both Merriam-Webster and Oxford English Dictionary editors added "olingo" to their next unabridged editions or supplements. Even more oddly, neither Goldman nor anyone else has been able to learn its tribal language of origin. Those who use it can only shrug and say they've heard it. So a reasonable guess is that early Spaniards combined their word for smelly—*oliente*—with a soon-forgotten Indian name such as *otorongo*, for "little honey-loving bears of the jungles who are not fierce like bigger bears."

Later, Germans borrowed an African name for lemurs to call the olingo a *maki-bär*, a name still used. And in Central America mico, a name for small monkeys, was passed along to kinkajous as *mico-león*, "lion monkey," and to olingos as *mico-gringo* because the soft upright fur on its crown looked like the crew-cut most Mexicans of the 1920s saw only on North Americans.

Colors and clues: In addition to previous descriptions, olingo tails are thicker furred than those of kinkajous and have dark brown rings which kinkajou tails lack. Body fur is usually browner, lacking the kinkajou's red-gold glow. The face is grayer, also. As with all this family, newborn young are darker than adults.

Size: Body is more slender than the kinkajou's, legs are longer (to give that extra agility). Overall nose-to-tail-tip length about the same (30 to 36 inches). Weight 3 to 5 pounds.

Range and habitat: In comparison to the kinkajou, does not go quite so far north into Mexico nor so far east on the

South American continent but does go much farther southwest all the way to Ecuador, Peru, Bolivia. Same rain-forest
habitat—and same threat from forest destruction.
Additional species: Allen's olingo, *Bassaricyon alleni*;
Beddard's olingo, *Bassaricyon beddardi*.

SUBFAMILY AILURINAE

Similarities: The two species in this group—red panda
and giant panda—are so different in appearance there
seems no valid reason for classifying them together. One is
medium-sized and plume-tailed, the other is huge and
stub-tailed. But scientific grouping is determined by other
factors, including the structure of the feet. And both pandas have unique foot structure among carnivores. Each has
a loosely-attached mound or lump of flesh beneath its
inmost toe on each forepaw—almost like a sixth finger or
an almost-thumb. The mound is actually an extension of
the wristbone, but its unique maneuverability makes it
more thumblike in use. The giant's mound is better developed, more agile, but the two are enough alike to serve as
the main reason the same red panda and giant panda share
subfamily status.

Both are granted alignment with the Procyoninae
because the raccoon's low-set toes give it much the same
maneuverability even though the actual structure is not
alike. No other family group in Order Carnivora comes
even close in foot structure.

Besides general appearance and foot structure, family
kinship is also based on actions, voice, jaw/teeth forma-
tion, genitalia, digestive process and infant size at birth.
Red pandas are like raccoons on 6 of these 8 points: general appearance, actions, voice, jaw/teeth, genitalia and
infant size. The giant panda is raccoonlike only in genitalia
and jaw/teeth, but that odd foot structure outweighs all
the rest at present. Perhaps in time, more precise knowledge of genes and chromosomes and other factors will
provide other criteria to determine kinship, but so far the

knowledge isn't established.

The subfamily name means "catlike" from Greek *ailuris*, a name for all medium-sized furry creatures with waving tails long before it became limited to felines. The red panda's plumed tail led to this choice, and since it was first of the two species to be classified, its generic label becomes the basis for any further family or subfamily designation. The strict rules of scientific nomenclature force the giant to share *ailuris* label even though there is nothing feline in its appearance. Many classifiers believe there is enough evidence even now to place it with the bears—a relationship granted in its homeland Himalayan hills long, long ago. But there is a general willingness to leave the red panda where it is instead of re-assigning it to the fox family as it was in ancient China and Nepal.

J.G. Wood, 1865.

PANDA, OR WAH.—*Ailurus Fulgens.*

RED PANDA, *Ailurus fulgens* (F. Cuvier) [France, 1825]
Early records: Both pandas first appeared on written record in a list of tribute payments demanded by the great Emperor Yu of China from his provincial warlords about

147

4000 years ago. This tribute roll survived the centuries and was eventually translated to other languages and prized as an historic document of great value. Actually, the list names "foxes of all kinds" but because the old Chinese name for the red panda was "fire-bright fox," it was surely included among the tribute pelts. The giant was there too, for the wording was "bears of all kinds, especially the great white one" and that phrase designates for the giant.

About 3000 years ago—1050 B.C.—another Chinese ruler, Emperor Wu Wang, created what he called a Park of Learning—a place where he could bring live wild animals together so he could watch and learn their ways. Both the "fire bright" and the "great white one" were among his collection.

The first European to see them must have been Marco Polo, for he returned to Italy in 1295 with tales of a white bear and a "different kind" of fox. No one thought these animals anything special. Polar bears had already been on record and foxes come in various colors. And since most Europeans traveling to Asia in later years were interested in gold and silk and spices, instead of foxes and bears, the two pandas had to wait another six centuries for discovery.

The red panda came to European attention first by nearly half a century. In 1821 a Nepalese hunter came to the Danish botanist Nathaniel Wallach in Calcutta with the pelt of an animal the Dane had never seen before in all his travels. He thought it handsome, especially the tail. But animals were not his specialty and so he passed it along to an English friend—soldier and amateur naturalist Major-General Thomas Hardwicke. The general was about to sail back to England and he happily took the pelt with him. First, however, he managed to learn all he could from another Englishman—Brian Hodgson—who said he'd known this redcoat in both Sikkim and Nepal. Its cry was so much like that of a human baby, he told Hardwicke, that Nepalese called it "baby," *wha*, or "mountain baby," *chit-wha*.

In London Hardwicke had the skin carefully mounted, and displayed it at a meeting of the London Linnean Society November 6, 1821. Members gathered around, exclaiming at the marvel of a species never before seen on the European continent. However, they were more than ready to reject so silly a name as *wha* no matter how authentic. "Himalayan raccoon" someone nominated, pointing to the masklike face markings. Others pointed to the tail and were equally insistent the name be "Himalayan fox".

Hardwicke, only an amateur at nature study, didn't realize he had to publish a name and description of this animal with proper details or lose credit for its discovery and official recognition. Before he could get such a project underway, a similar pelt arrived at the French national museum in Paris. There in charge were the Cuvier brothers—Frederic and George—who knew exactly what had to be done.

The French pelt had come from Alfred Duvaucel, a collector in India and nearby lands for several years. He'd wrapped up skin, jaw bones and one foot skeleton—all essential for classification—and sent a hurried note giving the local name of *panda* and rushed it off by the first mail boat for Europe, promising further details as soon as possible. They would never be written—for Duvaucel came down with a virulent tropic fever and soon died.

In Paris the Cuvier brothers were delighted with the challenge to get this new species on official lists before the laggard Englishman got around to it. They wished they knew the meaning of *panda*, and where Duvaucel had learned it, but they went ahead.

Frederic, in charge of classification, had no trouble choosing a binomial. "I propose *ailurus* for the generic name," he wrote, "because of the exterior likeness to the cat...and for species name, *fulgens*, because of its glowing color."

The Latin word means both "fire bright" and "shining"—a perfect match for both the glowing auburn fur and the old Chinese name. The full French label—*panda écla-tant*, "shining panda"—would soon be shortened to panda. After all, there was no other kind of panda in the whole world, they thought, so a descriptive term was not needed.

When the Cuviers finally learned of Duvaucel's death, they questioned everyone who had any knowledge of Nepalese dialects. Nobody had ever heard the name "panda." Not until much later would linguists suggest that Duvaucel had misheard the initial consonant. The word may have been *banda* or *bandhu*, stemming from ancient Tamil and Sanskrit names for the tie-and-dye process Himalayan women use to decorate kerchiefs, skirts and blouses with alternate bands of color. It is the root source for the word "band" as well as "bandanna" and now it seems just as clearly the source for "panda." The red panda's banded face and tail markings must have been the reason it was called this by the Nepalese. Oddly, no one except Duvaucel ever heard banda or panda as the name for *Ailurus fulgens*. Or perhaps not so oddly. Isolated tribes do have local terms. They also like to laugh, and the name Duvaucel heard could have been an old family joke—a woman's joke hunters never used.

Europeans in the Orient soon found the red panda in China as well as Nepal. There its name was *hun-ho*, "fire fox," or *hsiung maou*, "bear cat." Several other names would be added from different areas over the years, and travelers also learned that certain tribes paid the fire fox full respect as a spirit-being and copied its facial markings on the masks they wore in tribal rituals. Its meat was therefore taboo as food and only tribes of other beliefs used its fur for caps.

After the giant panda was named, the original panda needed an identifying adjective. Several were used including "shining panda" as Cuvier had originally labeled it, "true panda," "common panda"— because it was more abundant than the giant,— or "lesser panda" to mark its smaller size. But "lesser" also denotes lower quality, and the species that was the sole possessor of panda name for forty-five years should not be denigrated by a label that hints inferiority. Recently "red panda" has been preferred by many writers and zoo authorities who find *Ailurus fulgens* an appealing attraction even if it will never have the world-sweeping acclaim given the giant. On all counts it is very much worth knowing, and those who also know raccoons will see many likenesses.

Colors and clues: Masklike markings on the face are similar to a raccoon's but the eye-band is narrower with down-curved lines. Nostrils are black and prominent, the tail is bushy and ringed and the body fur has a glossy sheen and auburn glow.

Unlike raccoons, a red male has one mate only and is part of the family circle, often seen with mate and young. The den is a hollow tree or rocky cave. Usually two kits make a litter, but sometimes three or four are seen and they stay with the parents about ten months. They have divided sleeping times—two hours or so at midnight and another retreat at midday—with plenty of time in between for finding food.

Their menu includes fruit, insects, bulbs, roots, acorns, small rodents, birds and bird eggs as well as bamboo sprouts and tender tips. Their claws are good for digging and are semi-retractile. Their calls may be the namesake "wha-wha" wail or clipped whistles and squeaks, or even fiery hisses and snorts when danger threatens. Like all Procyonids there is a musky anal odor, but nothing like the olingo's stench.

Size: Adult length nose to tail tip is about 40 inches, nearly half of which is tail. Adult weight is given at 10 to 12 pounds—less than they look because most of their bulk is in thick fur. Kits weigh about 2 ounces at birth and rapidly gain size and strength, always ready to hiss defiance at any leopard trying to poke its nose in the den door.

Range and habitat: From Nepal, Sikkim, Bhutan, Assam,

Laos and Burma on to Chinese provinces of Yunan and Szechuan red pandas are at home in mountain forests at heights from 5,000 to 12,000 feet. Elsewhere they are seen only in captivity, except for occasional hunger raids in farmyards on lower slopes near the den.

The first red panda in a European zoo arrived in London in May of 1869 but lived only seven months. Even in that short time it had hundreds of visitors and posed for a color portrait as it nibbled on its favorite yellow berries. The first red panda in the United States was in the Bronx Zoo in 1911, where they are still favorites. The National Zoo also has red pandas and often loans a pair to other zoos with hope of producing zoo-born kits. A phone call to your local zoo will tell you where you'll find them.

Reds sleep during much of the zoo's visiting hours and so you may not see them in action or hear them call. But you can hear a recording of an adult whistle on the record accompanying the book *Animal Language* by Julian Huxley, published in England in 1938 and reprinted by Grosset & Dunlap in New York in 1964.

GIANT PANDA, *Ailuropoda melanoleuca* (Milne-Edwards) [France, 1870]

Encyclopaedia Britannica, 1909.

FIG. 6.—The Parti-coloured Bear, or Giant Panda
(*Aeluropus melanoleucus*).

Early records: Fossil bones of the giant found in southern China date its presence there some ten thousand years ago. Four thousand years ago it was named on the emperor's tribute list along with its smaller relative. A thousand years later both were in the emperor's Park of Learning, and both were in Marco Polo's journals of 1295.

Only the giant, however, was named in 625 A.D. when another emperor of China was forced to pay tribute to the victorious emperor of Japan who had heard of the great white one. Seventy fine pelts of this beast were sent to Japan along with the supreme offering of two live cubs. If they caused as much commotion as the first cubs seen in the United States, the emperor's court must have been in tumult that day. The Chinese characters on the scroll that accompanied the tribute gave the word "white" the phonic value of *pei* but it was also written *bei* in other documents. Sometimes this was followed by *hsiung,* meaning "bear," but not always.

The first modern European to see the giant panda definitely thought "bear" was part of the name. *Pai-shioug* was the way it was spelled phonetically in 1869 by a very excited and delighted Père Armand David, a French missionary priest visiting a mission school in Szechuan province when he heard of this rarity. It was seldom seen, he was told, but it did live nearby somewhere in the encircling mist-shrouded forests. Even a glimpse usually demanded a long and ardous search, but right then a neighbor had a pelt he was proud to display. At least the pelt would show Père David what to look for.

Father David was ready to start that minute, and as soon as permission was granted, he was gazing in awe and wonder at the huge pelt with its ink-black furry circles masking the black eyes.

"What a remarkable species!" he wrote in his diary that night. "What a find for science!" And he promptly hired hunters to bring him a pelt to send back to Paris so the National Museum could claim credit for first classification.

Amazingly, in only three weeks he had a pelt. Not the full-grown adult he'd hoped for, but the half-grown cub showed all the features needed for classification. Immediately he began taking measurements, writing down detailed descriptions of jawbone, teeth and—the most important feature—the odd hairy-soled forepaw with its maneuverable bump. He coined a binomial, of course, for he was a trained scientist as well as a priest, labeling it *Ursus melanoleucus*, "black-and-white bear."

Sure he had included everything museum experts would need for publication, he added a final postscript: "Publish now!" He feared someone else would give another nation the prestige of discovery if he waited for the pelt to arrive. A letter would travel much faster, for it could be carried to the coast by runners, while the hefty package with the skin and bones would have to go by slow ox cart.

In Paris Alphonse Milne-Edwards and other museum experts were as excited as Père David. But they decided to wait for the pelt so they would have actual proof if challenged. Luckily no one else was any earlier. Museum experts overruled David's classification and placed it with the panda because of its "thumb." So the binomial they published was *Ailuropoda melanoleuca*, "panda-footed one in black and white." And of course it was placed with the original panda in Family Procyonidae, not with the bears.

Father David wasn't the only scientist to disagree. The raccoon-or-bear argument is still going on among taxonomists. But when ordinary people in the outside world finally saw the pelt—and eventually the live giants—they called it a bear. Panda bear, they said at first glance—and still say it, whether live animals or cuddly plush toys are involved.

Colors and clues: The black circles around the giant's black eyes may be close enough to a raccoon mask to make a point for Procyonidae kinship. But the huge size and stub tail are obviously bearlike. Infant size is bearlike also. Red pandas and raccoons and the other species in Procyoninae all have young of the normal size for adult mammals of their weight. But newborn giants and bears are amazingly small.

A newborn giant panda, for instance, weighs only 4 to 5 ounces—about twice the size of a newborn red. But adult giants weigh from 250 to 300 pounds and so can be 15 or 20 times the bulk of adult red pandas. When a red mother picks up her kit to move it to safer quarters, you see the dangling baby plainly. When a giant mother picks up her ultra-small kit you can scarcely see either nose or rump extending beyond her lips. The baby isn't much bigger than her tongue.

Range and habitat: Giant pandas are at home in mountain bamboo forests from Szechuan and Yunan provinces in southern China north along Himalayan slopes to Tibet. Because of this multi-national range it has been called "Tibetan bear" as often as "Chinese" or "Himalayan bear." It has also been termed "clawed bear," "bamboo bear," "harlequin bear" and "particolored bear"—the last two for its black-and-white color scheme. Both American and British zoologists accepted the French choice of panda eventually. The British preferred "great panda" to "giant" but finally ceded to the Americans.

The first live giant panda seen anywhere outside the Orient was a kit called Su-Lin, "Little Cutie," brought to New York by way of San Francisco by Ruth Harkness, December 27, 1936. It was permanently acquired by the Brookfield Zoo just outside of Chicago on February 8, 1937, and remained there until its death in April 1938. For the last few months it had another giant panda playmate, Mei-Mei, "Pretty-Pretty," and all of us who had the joy of watching them play will never forget. Even the thousands who saw only photographs or plush toy copies were instantly enchanted, and newspaper reporters liked to describe this overwhelming affection as "panda-mania" or "panda-monium."

Everywhere live pandas bring the same instant enchantment—not only here in the United States but also in zoos in Tokyo, Mexico City, London, Moscow and Madrid as well as in China. Chinese zoos—and a few of the others—have been successful in producing live kits. But Ling-ling, "Dear Little Girl," and Hsing-hsing, "Star-Bright Boy," who came to our National Zoo in 1972 have so far not produced viable kits.

Recent years have seen increased concern for giant panda survival in the wild. In China—as almost everywhere these days—more and more wild acreage has been taken over by humans, leaving less and less untrammeled terrain where wild creatures can find food and shelter. Also some kinds of bamboo plants are dying out, bringing added threat of starvation to both pandas, especially the giant.

Because of the difficulty zoos have with breeding and rearing them, no more pandas in the wild could also mean no more pandas anywhere. Various conservation groups are working hard to find ways to offset this threat and may succeed.

ELEVEN

A SAMPLING OF RACCOON NAMES AND NAMESAKES

THE ORIGINAL NAMES FOR THE RACCOON and its closest relatives in Subfamily Procyoninae came from the tribal languages of Native Americans. All tribal names had descriptive meanings chosen to distinguish each kind of animal from others in some way. However, not all of those meanings have survived the centuries, and many of the names themselves have vanished from memory. Among those that eventually found written record are these:

Names describing agile forepaws
Abnaki: *asban*, one who lifts up things
Algonkin: *ah-rah-koon-em*, they rub, scrub, scratch
Atakapa: *welkol, (wilkol, wulkol, wutko),* they rub and scratch
Aztec: *mapachitl*, they take everything in their hands
Biloxi-Sioux: *atuki*, they touch things
Chinook: *q'oala's*, they scratch
Chippewa: *aasebun,* aissibun, they pick up things
Choctaw: *shauii*, graspers
Cree: *essebanes*, they pick up things
Creek: *wutku*, they rub and scratch

Delaware: *eespan*, one who picks up things;
  wtakalinch, one very clever with its fingers
Lenape: *eespan, hespan*, they handle things;
  nachenum, they use hands as a tool
Menomini: *aispan*, they handle things
Mohican: *sha-we*, grasper
Natick: *asban*, they pick up things
Ofo-Sioux: *at-cha*, one who touches things
Ojibway: *aispun, essepan*, they pick up things
Seminole: *wood-ko*, one who rubs
Shawnee: *shapata, ethepata*, grasper
Takelma: *swini*, picks up things with hands
Tschimshean: *que-o-koo*, washes with hands
Yakima: *k'alas*, they scratch

Names describing face
Dakota-Sioux: *weekah tegalega*, magic one with painted face
Hopi: *shiuaa*, painted one
Huron-Iroquois: *attigbro*, blackened (face);
  gahado-goka-gogosa, masked demon spirit
Mandan: *nashi*, blackened face and feet
Mexico (tribe not given): *macheelee*, white bands on face
Nicaragua (tribe not given): *macheelee*, white bands on face
Wyot: *cbel'igacocib*, one with marked face

Names implying magic (both sexes)
Cheyenne: *macho-on*, one who makes magic
Dakota Sioux: *wee-kah (wee-chah, wee-kahsah, wici, wicha)* one
  with magic; *wee-kah tegalega*, magic one with
  painted face (*or wici*)
Omaha, Osage, Otoe: *mee-kah, (mee-chah, mee-kahsa)*
  same meaning as *wee-chah* and variants one with magic
Sioux: *macca-n-e*, one who makes real magic
Yankton Sioux: *wayatcha* (same root word as *wee-kah*)

Names for females with magic
Mexico (used by Aztecs but probably borrowed from

another tribe):

see-o-ahtlah-ma-kas-kay (cioatlamacasque) she who talks with spirits; ee-yah-mah-tohn, she (little old one) who knows things

Yakima: tsa-ga-gla-lal, she who watches (legendary); witch, spirit

Names describing big tail (long tail, ringed tail)
Chinook: siah-opoots-itswoot, long-tailed bearlike one
Huron: ee-ree-ah-gee, those of big-tailed (long-tailed) kind
Iroquois: gah-gwah-gee, cah-hee-ah-gway, big (long) tailed ones
Sioux: shinte-gleska, ring-tailed ones
Seneca: kagh-quau-ga, big (long) tailed
Wyandot: ee-ree, big-tailed, long-tailed ones

Names comparing to dog
Arawak: ah-ohn, dog, of dog kind
Guyana: mayuato, doglike leaper
Huron-Iroquois: agaya, doglike one
Klamath: wacgina, tamed like dog
Narragansett: ausup, night doglike one
Taino: ah-ohn, ah-oon, of the dog kind
Tupi: aguara, doglike leaper

Names indicating eaters of crabs, crayfish
Choctaw: shauii, graspers (of crayfish)
Guyana: mayuato, doglike leaper on crabs and crayfish
Kiowa: seip-kuat, pulls out crayfish with hands (seip-mantei, crayfish)
Tupi: aguara-po-pay, doglike leaper on crabs, crayfish (used by other tribes in Tupi trade-jargon area)

Names for pelt only or sewn pelt garment
Algonkin: match-koh (for pelt or pelt sewn into poncho-type coat)
Algonkin-Roanoke: macquoc
Narragansett: mohewonck, pelt sewn into poncho-type

coat (*wonck*=coat)
Ojibway: *matchigode*, raccoon fur garment for women
Wocoon: *auher*
Alaska/Canada: *tsick-re-buck*, Indian version of *schupp/raccoon?*
Iroquois: *tschoe-ra-gak*, Indian version of schupp, used by
   traders asking first for schupp and then raccoon
   skins—neither word known to Indians?

Names without literal meanings
Blackfeet: *kaka-nostake*
Brazil: (tribe not given): *guassini, guachini*
Caddo: *o'at*
Canada (tribe not given): *ottaguin, ochateguin*
Iroquois: *tcokda*
Mikwok: *patkas*
Nez Perce: *kai-kai-yuts*
Nootka: *klapissime*
Pima: *va-owok*
Suislaw: *pilquits*
Taos: *pah-suh-de-na*, water?
Tillamook: *dEwu'si*, living raccoons; *wEluhs*, legendary
   raccoon
Tuscarora: *roosotto*
Tutelo: *kanulo-nixa-niso*

Non-Indian names
American-English: coon, rattoon
Canadian French: *chat, chat sauvage*, cat, European wildcat
Danish: *skjob*, fisher, fur trade name
Dutch: *schob*, fisher, fur trade name
French: *raton, raton laveur*, little rat, little washer rat
Finland: *siupp*, fisher, fur trade name
German: *schupp*, fisher, fur trade name, *waschbär*, washer
   bear from Linnaeus *Ursus lotor*
Latin: Linnaeus, *Systema Naturae*, 1747: *Ursus cauda elongata;*
   1748: *Ursus cauda annulata, fascia per oculos transversali;*
   1758: *Ursus lotor*

Latin: Hernández, Francisco, *Historiae Animalium...Novai Hispaniae*,1651: *cane melitensi*, badgerlike dog
Lithuanian: *sunluskis*, dog-bear
Polish: *szop*, fisher, fur trade name
Russian: *jenot*, fisher, fur trade name
Spanish: *mapache*, from Aztec, *mapachitli*, uses hands; *oso lavador*, washer bear (from Linnaeus); *perro mastin, mudo, tejón*, masked, barkless, badgerlike dog, popular usage
Swedish: *sjupp* fisher, fur trade name; *tvättbjörn*, from Linnaeus,washer bear

RACCOON NAMESAKES

Raccoons held such an important role in pioneer life, that they have many namesakes all across the land. On the coast, oysters that clung to the rocks close to shore were known as "raccoon oysters" because the mask wearers would be sure to get them before any humans had a chance. Inland fisherman called the yellow perch a "raccoon perch" because it so often made the furry fisherman a tasty meal. Wild grapes were "raccoon grapes" in folk speech and snowberries and several other wild berries were "raccoon berries" all for the same good reason.

Many raccoon namesakes are not only heard in everyday folk speech but are clearly printed on official maps from Raccoon Cay in the West Indies to Raccoon River in Iowa. Namesake towns and cities include Raccoon, Indiana; Raccoon Mills, Georgia; Coon Rapids, Iowa, and Coon Valley, Wisconsin. You can go fishing in Raccoon Creek in Arkansas, Illinois, Indiana, New Jersey, Ohio and Pennsylvania or in Coon Creek in Illinois, Michigan, Mississippi or Oklahoma. Raccoon Mountains are on the map in Alabama, Raccoon Point is in Louisiana, Coon Butte in Arizona, Coon River in Iowa and Raccoon Key in South Carolina. Raccoon Ford on the Rapidan River in Virginia is not only on the map but was twice the scene of

161

battle during the Civil War—first in 1862 and again in 1865. Some Indian names still have their namesakes on the map, too. Lake Erie may not be recognized by everyone as belonging on this list, but there's no doubt about *Rio Mapache* in Mexico. Very likely two place names in Florida—Wakulla County and the town of Wauchula—stem from the word *welkol* and its variants that meant raccoon in Atakapa, Creek and Seminole languages. Several others seem related to the name used by Sioux affiliates—*weecha* and variants—such as Wichita, Ouachita, Washita. Could the Taos name for raccoon—*pah-su-de-na*—somehow be the source for naming California's City of Roses? Is Atoka, Oklahoma, a namesake of *atuka*, Biloxi-Sioux for "those who touch things?"

Indian names are difficult to trace, but there's no doubt that *Rapides des chats* and *Lac des Chats* in Champlain's diaries and today's maps of Canada are marking raccoon presence. *Bahia de Perros* on Cuba's north shore may recall the first Spaniards' "badgerlike dogs" alias for raccoons. A search of your own local maps may add still more to the list of names that say, "Raccoons were here."

Photo: Noel Young

Photo: John Pitman

BIBLIOGRAPHY

Procyonines: History and General Background

Acosta, Jose de. *Naturall and Morall Historie of East and West Indies.*
London: Edward Grimston, 1604. (Original: Seville, 1590)

Allen, Joel. "Description of a new generic type Bassaricyon," *Proceedings
of the Academy of Natural Sciences of Philadelphia,* 1876, 1877.

Audubon, John James and John Bachman. *Imperial Collection of Audubon
Animals.* Maplewood, New Jersey: Hammond, Inc., 1967 (Original:
1845-1848)

Beechey, Frederick W. *Narrative of a Voyage 1825-1828.* London: Colburn
& Bentley, 1831.

Bernaldez, Andres. *Cronica de los reyes catolicos.* Madrid: *Coleccion Rosell,*
1953. (Original: c. 1539)

Bewick, Thomas. *General History of Quadrupeds.* London: 1790-1800.

Blunt, Wilfred. *Compleat Naturalist: A Life of Linnaeus.* New York: Viking
Press, 1971.

Breland, Keller & Marian. *Animal Behavior.* New York: Macmillan, 1966.

Buffon, Georges, comte de. *Histoire Naturelle.* Vols V & VI. Paris:
1749-1767.

Byrd, William. *Histories of the Dividing Line.* New York: Dover, 1967.
(Original : 1728)

Cahalane, Victor. *Mammals of North America.* New York: Macmillan,1947.

Cartier, Jacques. *Brief Recit.* in *Early English and French Voyages.* Henry S.
Burrage, ed. NewYork: Barnes & Noble, 1906.

Catesby, Mark. *Natural History of Carolina, Florida and the Bahama Islands.*
London: self-published, 1731-1743.

Champlain, Samuel. *Brief Discours . . . aux Indes Occidentallea . . . 1599-1601.*
Quebec: Laverdiere, 1870.

Champlain, Samuel. *Carte Geographique . . . 1612.* Harvard Library.

Colon, Fernando. *Life of the Admiral.* Translated by B. Keene. New
Brunswick, New Jersey: Rutgers University Press, 1959. Conn:
Greenwood Press, 1978. (Original: Venice, 1571)

Coma, Guillermo. "Letter to Niccolo Scillacio" or *De insulis
meridiani.* Pavia, Italy: 1494 or 1495.

Crandall, Lee. *A Zoo Man's Notebook.* Chicago: Univ. Press, 1966.

Dampier, William. *A New Voyage Around the World.* New York: Dover,
1968. (Original: 1697, 1729).

De Angleria, Pedro Martir. *De Orbe Novo: The Eight Decades of Peter
Martyr de Anghera.* Translated by T.A. MacNutt. NewYork:
G.P. Putnam's Sons, 1912. (Original: Italy, 1504 ff,Spain, 1511-1530)

De Armas, Juan Ignacio. *La zoologia de colon y de los primeros exploradores de Americas.* Cuba: Establacimento Tipografico O'Reilly, 1888.

DeBry, Theodore. *Collectiones Peregrinatium.* Frankfort, Germany: DeBry and Sons, 1590-1634.

DeBry, Theodore. *Brevis Narratio eorum quae en Florida,* 1591.

De Escalante Fontaneda, Hernando. *Memoir.* Coral Gables, Florida: Glade House, 1945. Translated by Buckingham Smith. Washington,D.C.: 1854 from original Spanish 1575.

Eckert, Alan. "Wild Season." *True,* May 1967. From *Wild Season,* Boston: Little, Brown, 1967.

Erdoes, Richard. "Sioux Medicine Men Still Work Wonders," *Argosy,* June, 1971.

Fowler, Melvin L. "Modoc Rock Shelter." *American Antiquity,* January, 1959, vol 24, # 3, pp. 250-270.

Gesner, Conrad. *Historia animalium.* Zurich, 1551.

Goldman, Edward A. *Mammals of Panama.* Washington, D.C.: Smithsonian Institution (Smithsonian Miscellaneous Collection, vol 60, # 2. 1912; volume 69, #5, 1920).

Grant, W.L. *Voyages of Samuel de Champlain.* New York: Scribners, 1907.

Hahn, Emily. *Animal Gardens.* New York: Doubleday, 1967.

Hall, E.R. and Kelson, K.R. *Mammals of North America.* New York: Ronald Press, 1959.

Hartman, Carl. *Possums.* Austin, Texas: University of Texas Press, 1932.

Heinold, George. *Burglar in the Treetops.* New York: Holt, 1952.

Hernández, Francisco. *Cuatro Libros de la Naturaleza y Virtudes Medicinales de la Plantas y Animales y Minerales de Nueva Espana Usados en la Medicina.* Mexico: 1615, 1888.

Hernández, Francisco. *Nova Plantarum, Animalium et Mineralim Mexicorum Historia.* Rome: 1651.

Holmgren, Virginia C. "Olingos and Kinkajous." *Americas.* August,1979.

Huet, Paul. *Novelles Archives du Musee D'Histoire Naturelle de Paris, 2m series, V:* Paris, 1883.

Jane, Cecil (tr.). *Journal of Christopher Columbus.* New York: Clarkson Potter, 1960.

Jardine, Sir William. *Naturalists' Library, Volume V, Mammals.* London/Edinburgh (no date: c.1858).

Johnson, Samuel. *Dictionary of the English Language.* London: eight editions, 1755-1799.

Josselyn, John. *An Account of Two Voyages: 1638-39, 1663-71.* London: Widdoes, 1674.

Josselyn, John. *New England Rarities.* London: Widdoes, 1672. (Reprint Boston: William Veazle, 1865, University Microfilm reel 980).

Kalm, Pehr. *Travels in North America.* New York: Dover, 1966. (Original: Stockholm, 1753; English, J.R. Forster, 1770; revised A. Benson, 1937).

Klein, Jacob. *Quadrupedes.* Lipsae (Lubec): 1751.

Las Casas, Bartolome. *Historia de Las Indias.* Madrid: 1875, 1951 (Original written 1559-61)

Lawson, John. *A New Voyage to Carolina.* London: 1709. (Reprint Chapel Hill, North Carolina: University of North Carolina Press, 1967)

Lewis, Meriwether and Clark, William. *Original Journals.* Reuben Thwaites, ed. New York: Dodd, Mead & Co., 1904-05. (Reprints: Antiquarian Press, 1959; Arno Press, 1969)

Linnaeus, Carl. *Systema Naturae.* Sweden: 10th edition, 1758; 12th edition, 1766.

Lumden, James. *Animals.* Glasgow: Lumden, 1794. (Facsimile reprint, New York: Hudson River Press, 1977.)

Lyell, Sir Charles. *Travels in North America.* Vol 1, p. 123. New York: 1845.

Manville, R.H. "Distribution of Alaskan Mammals." Washington, D.C.: U.S. Dept. of Interior Bulletin #211, 1965.

Marcgrave, Georg. *Historia Naturalis Brasiliae.* Amsterdam: 1648.

Mathews, M.M. (ed.). *A Dictionary of Americanisms.* Berkeley: University of California Press, 1958.

Michelson, Edward H. *Merchants Polyglot Manual.* London: Letts Son & Co., 1862.

Miller, G.S. and Kellogg, Remington. *List of N.A. Recent Mammals.* Washington, D.C.: U.S. National Museum Bulletin #205, 1955.

Mills, William C. "Exploration of the Tremper Mound." *Ohio Archaeological and Historical Quarterly.* Volume 25, 1916.

Morison, Samuel Eliot. *Journals and Other Documents on the Life and Voyages of Columbus.* New York: Heritage Press, 1963.

Morris, Desmond. *Mammals.* New York: Harper & Row, 1965.

North, Sterling. *Rascal.* New York: Dutton, 1963.

North, Sterling. *Raccoons Are the Brightest People.* New York : Dutton, 1966.

Otto, Martha Potter. "Masterworks in Pipestone: Treasures from Tremper Mound." *Timeline Magazine.* Volume 1, #1, Ohio Historical Society, 1984.

Oviedo y Valdez, Gonzalo Fernandez de. *De la natural hystoria de las Indias.* Toledo, Spain: 1526.

Oviedo y Valdez, Gonzalo Fernandez de. *Historia general y natural de las Indias.* Seville, Spain: 1537; Madrid, Spain: 1851.

Palmer, R. *Mammal Guide.* New York: Doubleday, 1954.

Peterson, R.L. *Mammals of Eastern Canada.* Toronto: University of Toronto Press, 1961.

Poglayen, Ivo. "Observations of Maki-bears in Captivity." Hamburg, Germany: 1965. Translated by Ursula R. Kuettner.

Purchas, Samuel. *Purchas, His Pilgrimes.* London: 1625. Glasgow: J. MacLehose & Sons reprint, 1905-7.

Redford, Polly. *Raccoons and Eagles.* New York: Dutton, 1965.

Richardson, Sir John. *Fauna Borealis Americana.* London: 1829.

Richardson, Sir John. *Quadrupeds.* New York: American Museum of Natural History, 1877.

Rue, Leonard. *World of the Raccoon.* New York: Lippincott, 1965.

Sahagún, Bernardino de. *Historia general de cosas de Nueva Espana.* Translated by C.E. Dibble and J.O. Anderson. Salt Lake City and Albuquerque: Presses of the Universities of Utah and New Mexico, 1963. (Original: c. 1560)

Sanderson, Ivan. *Living Mammals of the World.* New York: Doubleday, 1955.

Sanderson, Ivan. *How to Know the American Mammals.* Boston: Little, Brown, 1951.

Schoolcraft, Henry R. *Indian Legends from Algic Researches.* New York: Harper, 1839; Michigan State University Press, 1956.

Scott, W.B. *A History of Land Mammals in the Western Hemisphere.* New York: Hafner, 1932, 1967.

Seton, Ernest Thompson. *Lives of Game Animals.* Boston: C.T. Branford Co., 1909, 1926.

Smith, Captain John. *Generall Historie of Virginia, New England and the Summer Isles.* London: Michael Sparkes, 1624. Facsimile, Cleveland: World Publishing Co., 1966.

Stewart, George. *Names on the Land.* Boston: Houghton Mifflin, 1945.

Swainson, William. *Animals in Menageries.* London: Cabinet Cyclopedia, 1838.

Thevet, André. *Les Singularités de La France Antarctique.* Paris: 1557.

Thevet, André. *Newfound World or Antartike.* Translated by Thomas Hackett. London: 1568.

Thwaites, Reuben G. *Jesuit Relations.* Cleveland: Burrows Bros., 1900.

Thwaites, Reuben G. *Early Western Travels.* Cleveland: A.H. Clark Co., 1904-06.

Vespucci, Amerigo. *Quattuor Americi Navigationes.* American Culture Series A, 96, #1. (Original: 1504, 1507)

Wendt, Herbert. *Out of Noah's Ark.* Boston: Houghton Mifflin, 1959.

Wood, William. *New Englands Prospects.* London: 1634. (Microfilm: English Books 1475-1640, reel 980)

PROCYONINES: INDIAN NAMES AND LEGENDS

Arno Hermanos. *Catalogo de las Voces Usuales de Aimara, Castellao y Quechua.* La Paz, Bolivia: 1944.

Barker, M.A.R. *Klamath Dictionary.* Berkeley: University of California Press, 1963.

Bartlett, John R. *A Dictionary of Americanisms.* New York: Bartlett, 1848.

Beall, Tom. *Legends of the Nez Perce.* Lewiston, Idaho: no date. (Reprint from *Lewiston Morning Tribune,* various editions, 1935)

Boas, Frank. *Handbook of American Indian Languages.* Washington, D.C.: Bureau American Ethnology, #40, 1911.

Boas, Frank. *Vocabulary of the Chinook Indians.* New York: Aca. Sci, 1904.

Brinton, Daniel and Albert Anthony. *Lenape-English Dictionary.* Philadelphia: Historical Society of Pennsylvania. 1888.

Broadbent, Sylvia. *Southern Sierra Languages.* Berkeley: University of California Press, 1964.

Cook, Captain James. *Voyage to Pacific.* London: 1784.
Corse, Carita D. and Chestnutt, Felicia. *Indian Seminole Glossary.*
Unpublished ms. in Dade County, Florida, Public Librar, 1938.
Frachtenberg, Leo. "Contributions to Tutelo Vocabulary." *American Anthropologist,* 15: 477.
Gatschet, Albert and Swanton, John. *Dictionary of the Atakapa.*
Washington, D.C.: Smithsonian Bulletin # 108, 1922.
Goshe, Frederick. *Sioux Indian Language.* Valparaiso, Indiana: self-published, 1965.
Gudger, E.W. "George Marcgrave, First Student of American Natural History." *Popular Science Monthly,* September 1912, pp. 250-274.
Gudger, E.W. "Does Jaguar Fish With Its Tail?" *Journal of Mammalogy,* vol. 27: 37-49, 1946.
Hale, Horatio. "Tutelo Language." *Proceedings of American Philosophical Society,* March 2, 1883.
Hariot, Thomas. *A Brief and True Report.* New York: R. Adams, 1951. (Original, London 1588)
Heady, Eleanor. *Tales of the Nimipoo.* New York: World, 1970.
Hibben and Carswell. *Dictionary of Indian Tongues.* Victoria, B.C.: 1862. (Tshimpsean, Hydah, Chinook)
Loring, J. Malcolm and Louise. *Pictographs and Petroglyphs of the Oregon Country.* Los Angeles: University of California Press, 1982-83.
Lyell, Sir Charles. *Travels in North America.* Vol 1, p. 123. New York: 1845.
McCormick. S.J. *Dictionary of the Nez Perces.* Portland, Or: 1862.
Mahr, August C. "Delaware Terms for Plants and Animals." *Anthropological Linguistics,* volume 4, #5, May, 1962.
Molina, Alonso de. *Compendia del arte de la lengua Mexicana.* Puebla, Mexico: 1571. (Reprint with additions by Carochi & Paredes, 1759; revised 1910)
Rasles, Sebastien. *Dictionary of the Abnaki.* Cambridge, Mass: 1833.
Schoolcraft, Henry. *Indian Legends from Algic Research.* New York: Harper, 1839.
Stewart, George. *Names on the Land.* Boston: Houghton, Mifflin, 1945.
Stoutenburgh, John. *Dictionary of the American Indian.* New York: Crown, 1960.
Trumbull, James H. *Natick Dictionary.* Washington, D.C.: Smithsonian Bulletin #25, 1903.
U.S. Bureau of Ethnology. *Annual Reports,* 1879-1916
U.S. Geological Survey. *Rocky Mt. Region.* Vol VII, 1890.
Vasquez de Espinosa, Antonio. *Compendium and Description of the Indies.* Translated by Charles Clark. Washington, D.C.: Smithsonian, 1948. (Original c. 1620)
Williams, John H. *Guardians of the Columbia.* Tacoma, Washington: self-published, 1912.
Williams, Roger. *A Key to the Languages of America.* Detroit: Wayne State Univ. Press, 1973. (Original: 1643)
Zeisburger, William. *Indian Dictionary.* Cambridge, Mass.: Wilson, 1887.

Brock, Stanley. "East Meets West." *International Wildlife,* July-August 1972. Washington, D.C.: National Wildlife Federation.

Cox, C. *Sketches in Natural History.* Volume 1, "History of the Mammalia." London: C. Cox, 1849.

Gray, Betty. "Care and Development of a Hand-reared Panda at the National Zoo, Washington, D.C." *International Zoo Yearbook, 1970,* pp. 139-142. London: Zoological Society of London, 1970.

Hahn, Emily. *Animal Gardens.* New York: Doubleday, 1967.

Holmgren, Virginia C. "The Other Panda." *Animal Kingdon,* October, 1972.

Hinton, M. and Finn, Frank (eds.). *Hutchinson's Animals of All Countries.* Volume 1. London: Hutchinson and Co., no date.

Huxley, Julian and Koch, Ludwig. *Animal Language.* New York: Grosset & Dunlap, 1964. (Includes recording of red panda's voice.)

International Zoo Yearbook, yearly census of pandas in zoos. London: Zoological Society of London.

Jardine, Sir William. *Naturalists' Library.* Vol 15. London: 1858.

Morris, Desmond. *The Mammals.* New York: Harper & Row, 1965.

Morris, Desmond and Ramona. *Men and Pandas.* New York: McGraw-Hill, 1966.

Perry, Richard. *The World of the Giant Panda.* New York: Taplinger, 1969.

Polo, Marco. *Travels of Marco Polo.* Chapter 20. New York: Modern Library Editions.

Reed, Theodore. "Those Popular Pandas." *National Geographic,* Dec., 1972.

Richardson, Sir John. *Quadrupeds.* New York: American Museum of Natural History, 1877.

Sarich, Vincent, Wang Sung and LuChang-kun. "Giant Pandas in the Wild . . . and in a Biochemical Laboratory." *Natural History,* Dec., 1973.

Schaller, George B. "Secrets of the Giant Panda." *National Geographic,* March, 1986.

Swainson, William. *Natural History and Classification of Quadrupeds.* London: Cabinet Cyclopedia, 1835.

Wendt, Herbert. *Out of Noah's Ark.* Boston: Houghton, Mifflin, 1959.

Wood, John George. *The Illustrated Natural History.* London: George Routledge & Sons, 1865.

Author's personal observation of giant pandas from Brookfield Zoo, St. Louis Zoo, Bronx Zoo and of red pandas at the Washington Park Zoo, Portland, Oregon.

Personal correspondence with Theodore Reed, Director National Zoo; Charles O. Handley, curator and supervisor Division of Mammals, National Zoo; Ivo Poglayen, Director Louisville Zoo; Herbert

Penzyl, linguist, University of California, Berkeley; Georgette Dorn, Latin-American specialist, Library of Congress; Charles E. Dibble of the University of Utah; and Admiral Samuel E. Morison who graciously acknowledged he was "quite overwhelmed" by the author's data on raccoons and their dog misnomer.

INDEX

KEYBOARDED BY KATIE DABNEY, 1989.